THE COMMUNICATIONS HANDBOOK FOR INDIAN UNIVERSITIES

DR. DIVYA GUPTA

To the educators, communicators, and visionaries who shape the future of
higher education,
To the students whose curiosity and ambition inspire innovation,
And to my family, friends, and mentors, whose unwavering support and belief
have made this journey possible.

This book is for you. May it serve as a guide, a resource, and a reminder of the
transformative power of connection and communication.

Contents

Contents

Contents

Preface

In the rapidly evolving landscape of higher education, effective communication has become a cornerstone of institutional success. Universities today are not just centers of learning; they are dynamic ecosystems engaging diverse stakeholders—students, faculty, alumni, parents, industry partners, and society at large. For Indian universities, this role is even more pronounced, given the diversity, scale, and unique challenges of the higher education sector in India.

This handbook, The Communications Strategy Handbook for Indian Universities, is designed to equip university administrators, communications professionals, and academic leaders with practical tools, strategies, and insights to navigate the complexities of modern communications. From understanding the nuances of audience segmentation to leveraging cutting-edge technologies like artificial intelligence, this guide offers a comprehensive framework to enhance engagement, build reputation, and foster trust.

We have taken a holistic approach, addressing all facets of university communications—internal and external, digital and traditional, strategic and tactical. The content is enriched with best practices, case studies, and actionable templates, making it a valuable resource whether you're crafting a new communications strategy or refining an existing one.

Above all, this handbook recognizes the transformative power of education and the role of communication in amplifying its impact. By connecting voices, ideas, and communities, universities can inspire change, empower individuals, and contribute to a better future.

I hope this handbook serves as a trusted companion in your journey to elevate your university's communications. Let it guide you, challenge you, and inspire you to tell your story in ways that resonate and endure.

Warm regards,
Dr. Divya Gupta
Author

Prologue

Communication is the lifeblood of any institution, but in universities, it takes on an even greater significance. Here, communication shapes the exchange of ideas, fosters collaboration, and strengthens the bonds of community. It bridges the gap between diverse groups—students, faculty, alumni, administrators, and the wider society—ensuring that the institution's mission resonates with every stakeholder.

For Indian universities, this role is magnified. Situated in one of the most dynamic and diverse educational ecosystems in the world, they face unique challenges and opportunities. From addressing multilingual audiences to leveraging cutting-edge technologies, and from preserving cultural heritage to competing on a global stage, Indian universities must craft communication strategies that are both innovative and inclusive.

This handbook begins with a simple premise: communication is not just about broadcasting information; it is about building relationships and fostering trust. The strategies and tools shared within these pages are meant to empower universities to tell their stories, inspire action, and create lasting impact.

Whether you're a communications professional, an academic leader, or an administrator, this handbook is for you. It is a guide to navigating the complexities of modern university communications while remaining rooted in the values and vision of your institution. It is also a call to action—to embrace the power of communication to shape the future of higher education in India.

As you embark on this journey, remember that the heart of communication lies in connection. With each message you craft and each story you share, you are contributing to the legacy of education, shaping minds, and inspiring progress.

Welcome to the world of transformative communication. Let's begin.

Introduction To The Handbook

This comprehensive guide is designed to empower universities across India with the knowledge, strategies, and tools necessary to develop and execute effective communication plans. As the landscape of higher education becomes increasingly competitive and digitalized, the ability to communicate effectively with all stakeholders—students, faculty, alumni, and the public—has never been more critical.

Purpose of the Handbook

The primary aim of this handbook is to serve as a practical resource for university administrators, communication professionals, and academic leaders. It provides a step-by-step guide on crafting and implementing a communications strategy that aligns with the university's goals, enhances its reputation, and fosters a sense of community among all stakeholders.

The Importance of Effective Communication

In the context of Indian universities, effective communication plays a pivotal role in navigating the unique challenges and leveraging the opportunities within the higher education sector. Whether it's attracting prospective students, engaging current students and faculty, connecting with alumni, or promoting research and achievements, a well-thought-out communications strategy is vital.

Key Features of the Handbook

Comprehensive Coverage: From understanding the communications landscape to measuring the success of your strategies, the handbook covers all aspects of communications for Indian universities.

Practical Strategies and Tools: Each chapter is packed with actionable strategies, best practices, and recommendations for tools and technologies that can streamline and enhance your communications efforts.

Contextual Insights: Recognizing the unique cultural and educational context of India, the handbook provides tailored advice that addresses the specific needs and challenges of Indian universities.

Real-world Case Studies: Learn from the successes and setbacks of real-world communications campaigns within the Indian higher education sector.

How to Use This Handbook

This handbook is designed to be flexible, allowing readers to navigate to sections most relevant to their current needs and challenges. Whether you are developing a communications strategy from scratch or looking to enhance an existing plan, you will find valuable insights and guidance. We encourage you to use the templates and checklists provided in the appendices to facilitate planning and execution.

With the right approach to communication, universities can significantly enhance their impact, reputation, and the overall educational experience. We hope this handbook will be a valuable asset in your journey towards more effective communication. Here's to building stronger connections within your university community and beyond.

The Importance Of Effective Communication In Higher Education

In the dynamic and diverse landscape of higher education, particularly within the vibrant context of Indian universities, effective communication stands as a cornerstone for achieving institutional goals and fostering a thriving academic community. This section delves into the multifaceted role of communication in higher education, highlighting its significance in enhancing student experience, building relationships, and navigating the complexities of the modern educational environment.

Enhancing the Student Experience

At the heart of any university's mission is the student experience. Effective communication ensures that students are well-informed, engaged, and feel a sense of belonging to their university community. From orientation through to graduation, clear and consistent communication helps students navigate academic requirements, access support services, and take advantage of extracurricular opportunities. Moreover, in an era where digital platforms dominate, adapting communication strategies to meet students on their preferred channels is essential for fostering engagement and participation.

Facilitating Academic Success

Communication within the academic realm is not just administrative; it underpins the very essence of learning and teaching. Professors, lecturers, and academic staff need to convey complex ideas in clear, understandable ways. Additionally, fostering an environment where students feel comfortable expressing ideas and asking questions is crucial for academic discourse and learning. Effective communication skills are also vital for students, preparing them for success both within and beyond the university.

Building and Maintaining Relationships

Universities are ecosystems of relationships among students, faculty, alumni, and external stakeholders such as industry partners and the broader community. Effective communication nurtures these relationships, ensuring that alumni remain engaged and supportive, that collaborations with industry are fruitful, and that the university's contributions to society are well-communicated and understood. In this way, communication is a bridge connecting the university's past, present, and future.

Navigating Change and Crisis Management

The ability to communicate effectively is never more tested and crucial than during times of change or crisis. Whether dealing with public health concerns, shifts in educational policy, or internal challenges, how a university communicates can significantly impact its ability to navigate these issues successfully. Transparency, timeliness, and empathy in communication foster trust and confidence among all university stakeholders.

Enhancing Reputation and Competitiveness

In a competitive higher education landscape, a university's reputation is a pivotal factor in attracting and retaining talented students and faculty, as well as securing funding and research opportunities. Effective communication plays a key role in shaping perceptions, highlighting achievements, and articulating the university's values and vision. A well-crafted communications strategy amplifies the institution's strengths and differentiates it in a crowded marketplace.

The importance of effective communication in higher education cannot be overstated. It is a critical enabler for achieving educational excellence, building community, navigating challenges, and securing a university's place in the global educational landscape. For Indian universities, with their rich traditions and diverse student bodies, honing communication strategies is essential for unlocking their full potential and ensuring that they continue to thrive in an ever-evolving educational environment.

How To Use This Handbook

"The Communications Handbook for Indian Universities" is designed to be an accessible, comprehensive guide for enhancing the communications capabilities of universities across India. Whether you are a seasoned communications professional, an academic leader, or involved in the administrative aspects of higher education, this handbook offers valuable insights and practical advice tailored to your needs. Here's how to make the most of it:

Start with the Overview

Read the Introduction: Gain an understanding of the handbook's objectives, the importance of effective communication in higher education, and how this resource can be applied to your institution's unique context.

Familiarize Yourself with the Table of Contents: This will give you a broad overview of the topics covered and how the handbook is organized, allowing you to navigate to sections that are most relevant to your current priorities or challenges.

Tailor Your Approach

Identify Your Immediate Needs: Are you crafting a communications strategy from scratch, looking to improve digital engagement, or seeking guidance on crisis communication? Direct your attention to the chapters that address your specific concerns.

Use the Templates and Checklists: Appendices include ready-to-use templates and checklists for communications planning, execution, and evaluation. These tools are designed to streamline your processes and ensure nothing is overlooked.

Engage with the Content

Dive Deep into Specific Sections: Each chapter provides in-depth coverage of different aspects of communications strategy. Even if some sections are not immediately relevant, gaining a comprehensive understanding will benefit your overall strategy.

Review Case Studies: Real-world examples and case studies offer insights into successful strategies and common pitfalls. These narratives can provide inspiration and practical lessons for your own communications efforts.

Implement and Iterate

Apply Best Practices: Implement the strategies, tips, and best practices outlined in the handbook. Adapt these recommendations to fit the culture, needs, and objectives of your university.

Measure and Adjust: Utilize the guidance provided on measuring the effectiveness of your communications efforts. Use this data to make informed adjustments to your strategy, improving over time.

Keep It Handy for Reference

Refer Back Often: Communications strategies should evolve to meet changing needs, technologies, and stakeholder expectations. Keep the handbook accessible for quick reference, refresh your understanding, or inspire new initiatives.

Share with Colleagues: Effective communication is a collaborative effort. Share this handbook with colleagues across departments to ensure a cohesive and coordinated approach to your university's communications.

This handbook is more than just a resource—it's a companion in your journey to enhance the efficacy and impact of your university's communications. By understanding its contents, applying its advice, and adapting its strategies to your context, you can significantly contribute to the success and growth of your institution.

About The Author

Dr. Divya Gupta is a distinguished professional whose expertise spans the fields of photography, media, and communications. A TEDx speaker and the author of three acclaimed books, Divya's multifaceted career reflects a seamless blend of creativity, academic rigor, and industry insight. She is a two-time National Award-winning photographer whose work has earned widespread recognition and numerous accolades, both in professional and academic circles.

Currently serving as the Head of Communications at IES, Bangalore, Divya brings over seven years of rich experience in the education and media industries. Her past roles include Professor of Practice and Head of Creative Communications at IFIM Institutions, where she was instrumental in shaping innovative communication strategies. She has also worked with prominent institutions like O.P. Jindal Global University heading communications at the Office of the Vice Chancellor and Jagran Lakecity University, Bhopal, contributing significantly to their academic and administrative excellence.

Divya's commitment to the art and craft of photography has been a hallmark of her career. She has conducted numerous workshops, competitions, and exhibitions, inspiring the next generation of creative talent. Her work has been featured in prestigious newspapers and magazines, highlighting her impact as both an academician and a practitioner.

With a career defined by a passion for storytelling, Divya has consistently demonstrated the transformative power of communication. Through her books, lectures, and professional endeavors, she continues to inspire, educate, and empower others to harness the potential of creative expression in all its forms.

Copyright

Section 1 - Understanding the Communications Landscape in Indian Universities

CHAPTER ONE

Overview of Indian Higher Education

The Indian higher education system is one of the largest in the world, characterized by its vast diversity in terms of types of institutions, disciplines, and modes of delivery. With a rich heritage that dates back to ancient centers of learning like Nalanda and Takshashila, today's system has evolved to serve a burgeoning young population, making education both a priority and a challenge for the country. This overview provides a snapshot of the current landscape, highlighting the complexities, achievements, and challenges faced by Indian higher education today.

The Structure of Indian Higher Education

Central and State Universities: These are established by the government, with central universities funded by the Union government and state universities funded by the respective state governments.

Private Universities: These institutions have grown significantly in number and size, contributing to the expansion of higher education in India.

Deemed Universities: Institutions that enjoy the same academic status and privileges as a university but are a grade lower in terms of accreditation.

Institutes of National Importance (INIs): These are high-performing institutions in science, technology, engineering, and medicine, receiving special recognition and funding from the government.

Colleges: Affiliated with universities, these institutions primarily focus on undergraduate education, with some offering postgraduate courses.

Enrollment and Access

With over 44.5 million students enrolled in higher education, India has one of the largest student populations globally. The government has implemented several initiatives to increase enrollment rates, achieving a gross enrollment ratio (GER) of 33.1% by 2023-24. Efforts to promote inclusivity and access for underrepresented groups, including women and rural populations, are ongoing challenges that require innovative solutions.

Quality and Accreditation

The quality of higher education varies widely across institutions. The National Assessment and Accreditation Council (NAAC) and the National Board of Accreditation (NBA) are two key bodies responsible for maintaining educational standards. However, ensuring consistent quality across such a vast and diverse system remains a significant challenge.

Focus on Research and Innovation

Indian universities and institutes are increasingly emphasizing research and innovation. Initiatives like the National Institutional Ranking Framework (NIRF) encourage institutions to improve their research output and innovation capabilities. Yet, compared to global standards, Indian institutions have room to grow in terms of research impact and innovation.

Challenges

Funding and Infrastructure: Adequate funding and modern infrastructure are essential for quality education, yet many institutions face shortages in both areas.

Faculty Recruitment and Retention: Attracting and retaining qualified faculty members is a perennial challenge, impacting the quality of education and research.

Regulatory Environment: The higher education sector in India is highly regulated, which can sometimes hinder innovation and responsiveness to market demands.

Future Directions

The Indian government has launched several reforms aimed at overhauling the higher education system, including the National Education Policy (NEP) 2020. The policy proposes significant changes, including the introduction of a four-year multidisciplinary undergraduate program, greater flexibility in course choices, and an increased focus on research and innovation. The goal is to transform Indian higher education into a more holistic, flexible, multidisciplinary system that is aligned with the needs of the 21st century.

The landscape of Indian higher education is complex and diverse, with significant achievements and formidable challenges. As the system continues to evolve, it remains a critical component of India's development strategy, with the potential to shape the future of its youth and the country as a whole.

CHAPTER TWO

Key Challenges in University Communications

University communications play a pivotal role in shaping the reputation, reach, and effectiveness of higher education institutions. However, navigating the communications landscape, especially within the diverse and dynamic context of Indian universities, presents a unique set of challenges. These challenges stem from a variety of factors, including the sheer size of the target audiences, the diversity of these audiences, and the rapid evolution of communication technologies. Understanding these challenges is the first step toward developing effective strategies to address them.

1. Audience Diversity

Indian universities serve a wide range of stakeholders, including current and prospective students, faculty, staff, alumni, parents, and government bodies. Each group has distinct needs, preferences, and expectations from the university's communications. Crafting messages that resonate with this diverse audience, while maintaining a consistent voice and brand identity, requires nuanced understanding and strategic segmentation.

2. Balancing Traditional and Digital Channels

With the digital revolution transforming how information is consumed, universities face the challenge of integrating traditional communication channels with emerging digital platforms. Balancing these channels to ensure comprehensive reach and engagement can be daunting. Digital literacy among staff, resource allocation, and keeping pace with rapidly changing digital trends compound this challenge.

3. Crisis Communication

Universities are not immune to crises, ranging from natural disasters and health emergencies to reputational issues. The challenge lies in managing these crises effectively through timely, transparent, and empathetic communication. Developing and executing a crisis communication plan that protects the institution's reputation while addressing stakeholders' concerns is a complex task.

4. Resource Constraints

Many Indian universities operate under tight budget constraints, which can limit their communication efforts. Allocating funds for communication infrastructure, technology, and skilled personnel competes with other critical needs, such as teaching resources and research funding. This often results in underdeveloped communication departments and outdated strategies.

5. Keeping Up with Technological Advancements

The pace of technological change presents a challenge for university communications. New platforms, tools, and technologies emerge regularly, offering new ways to engage with audiences. However, adopting these technologies requires continuous learning, flexibility, and investment. Universities must navigate these changes to stay relevant and effective in their communication strategies.

6. Measuring the Impact of Communications

Determining the effectiveness of communication strategies is crucial for continuous improvement. However, accurately measuring this impact, especially in terms of qualitative outcomes like brand perception and stakeholder engagement, is challenging. Establishing clear metrics and investing in analytics tools are necessary but often overlooked due to resource constraints.

7. Regulatory and Ethical Considerations

Indian universities must navigate a complex regulatory environment that impacts their communication strategies. Ensuring compliance with government policies and ethical guidelines, while also engaging in open and transparent communication, requires diligent oversight and strategic planning.

8. Internal Communication

Effective internal communication is essential for fostering a positive organizational culture and ensuring that faculty, staff, and students are informed and engaged. However, creating an internal communication strategy that is both inclusive and efficient is a challenge, particularly in large institutions with diverse faculties and departments.

Addressing these challenges requires a strategic approach, leveraging both creative solutions and technological innovations. By recognizing and understanding the multifaceted nature of these challenges, Indian universities can develop more effective, responsive, and inclusive communication strategies that support their goals and enhance their impact on students, faculty, and society at large.

CHAPTER THREE

Recent Trends and Developments

The landscape of university communications is continually evolving, influenced by technological advancements, changing societal expectations, and the dynamic nature of higher education itself. Recognizing and adapting to these trends is crucial for universities to maintain relevance, engage effectively with their stakeholders, and navigate the complexities of the digital age. Below are some of the significant recent trends and developments in university communications, particularly relevant to the Indian context.

1. Digital and Social Media Dominance

Digital and social media platforms have become central to university communications strategies. These platforms offer unprecedented opportunities for engagement, allowing universities to reach wider audiences more efficiently than ever before. Content strategies now heavily focus on multimedia (videos, podcasts, interactive posts) that can be easily shared and consumed across devices, increasing the institution's visibility and engagement.

2. Personalization and Segmentation

With the abundance of data and sophisticated analytics tools available, universities are moving towards more personalized communication strategies. By segmenting their audiences based on interests, behaviors, and demographics, institutions can tailor their messages to meet the specific needs and preferences of each group. This approach enhances the effectiveness of communication campaigns, improving engagement and response rates.

3. Emphasis on Storytelling

Storytelling has emerged as a powerful tool in university communications. By sharing compelling stories of student achievements, faculty research, alumni success, and community impact, institutions can create emotional connections with their audiences. This not only helps in showcasing the university's contributions and successes but also strengthens the institution's brand and identity.

4. Crisis Communication and Reputation Management

In an era where information spreads rapidly, and public opinion can shift quickly, the ability to manage crises effectively has become more critical than ever. Universities are increasingly focusing on developing comprehensive crisis communication plans that include proactive measures, real-time monitoring, and rapid response strategies to protect and manage their reputation during challenging times.

5. Increased Focus on Accessibility and Inclusivity

Communications strategies are increasingly being designed with a focus on accessibility and inclusivity, ensuring that all content is available and understandable to diverse audiences, including those with disabilities. This shift not only reflects a commitment to social responsibility but also broadens the reach of university communications.

6. Integration of Artificial Intelligence and Automation

Artificial intelligence (AI) and automation technologies are being integrated into communication strategies to enhance efficiency and personalization. AI-driven chatbots for instant messaging, automated email marketing campaigns, and predictive analytics for audience engagement are examples of how universities are leveraging technology to streamline communications and improve user experiences.

7. Strategic Use of Data Analytics

Data analytics plays a crucial role in shaping university communications strategies. By analyzing engagement metrics, audience feedback, and campaign performance data, institutions can make informed decisions about their communications approaches, optimize campaigns in real-time, and demonstrate the ROI of their communications efforts.

8. Sustainability and Social Responsibility

There is a growing trend towards highlighting sustainability and social responsibility initiatives in university communications. As societal awareness and expectations around these issues increase, universities are using their platforms to showcase their commitment to sustainable practices, community engagement, and positive social impact.

These trends and developments reflect a broader shift towards more strategic, data-driven, and technologically sophisticated communications practices in higher education. For Indian universities, staying abreast of these trends is essential for enhancing engagement, building strong relationships with stakeholders, and navigating the rapidly changing communications landscape.

Section 2 – Setting Up Your Communications Foundation

CHAPTER FOUR

Establishing Your Communications Objectives

For universities, especially within the dynamic and diverse educational landscape of India, establishing clear and strategic communications objectives is pivotal. These objectives form the backbone of any effective communications strategy, guiding activities, and ensuring that every message aligns with the institution's broader goals and values. Below is a comprehensive guide to setting robust communications objectives that can elevate the stature and impact of Indian universities.

Understanding the Importance of Clear Objectives

Communications objectives are not just about promoting the university; they're about creating meaningful engagement with various stakeholders, including students, faculty, alumni, and the wider community. Clear objectives help to focus efforts, allocate resources efficiently, and measure the success of communications activities. They should be directly linked to the university's mission and strategic goals, ensuring that communications efforts contribute to the overall success of the institution.

Steps to Establish Effective Communications Objectives

1. Align with Institutional Goals: Begin by reviewing the university's strategic plan and goals. Your communications objectives should support these broader aims, whether it's enhancing the university's reputation, increasing student enrollment, engaging alumni, or supporting fundraising efforts.

2. Identify Key Audiences: Clearly define who your communications efforts will target. Different stakeholders may require different approaches. Understanding your audience's needs, preferences, and behaviors is crucial for crafting effective messages.

3. Assess the Current Communications Landscape: Conduct an audit of your current communications efforts to identify strengths, weaknesses, opportunities, and threats. This can help inform your objectives by highlighting areas for improvement or innovation.

4. Define Specific, Measurable Objectives: Objectives should be SMART: Specific, Measurable, Achievable, Relevant, and Time-bound. For example, rather than a vague goal like "improve communication," aim for something more tangible, such as "increase our social media engagement rate by 20% within the next year."

5. Consider the Broader Context: Keep in mind the unique challenges and opportunities within the Indian higher education sector, including regulatory changes, digital transformation, and the need for inclusivity and accessibility.

6. Establish Key Performance Indicators (KPIs): Alongside each objective, define how success will be measured. KPIs can include metrics such as website traffic, social media engagement rates, email open rates, or the number of media mentions.

Examples of Communications Objectives for Indian Universities

Enhance Brand Visibility: To increase the university's visibility and reputation nationally and internationally through targeted media outreach and social media engagement.

Improve Stakeholder Engagement: To foster a stronger community by increasing engagement rates with students, alumni, and faculty by 30% over the next 12 months through more personalized and interactive communication channels.

Support Enrollment Goals: To contribute to a 10% increase in student enrollment for the next academic year by implementing a strategic digital marketing campaign.

Promote Research and Innovation: To highlight the university's research achievements and innovation through a monthly newsletter and dedicated social media campaigns, aiming to increase external funding by 20%.

Crisis Communication Preparedness: To develop and implement a comprehensive crisis communication plan that ensures timely and transparent communication during emergencies, minimizing negative impacts on the university's reputation.

Setting clear, strategic communications objectives is a critical first step in developing an effective communications strategy for Indian universities. By aligning these objectives with the institution's broader goals, understanding the target audiences, and establishing measurable metrics for success, universities can significantly enhance their communications efforts, fostering a stronger, more engaged university community.

CHAPTER FIVE

Identifying Your Target Audiences

An essential step in crafting an effective communications strategy for any university involves identifying and understanding the target audiences. A well-defined audience helps tailor messages, select appropriate channels, and determine the best tactics for engagement. Indian universities, with their diverse stakeholder groups, must navigate a complex web of interests and needs. Here are key considerations and steps to identify your target audiences effectively.

Step 1: List Potential Stakeholder Groups

Start by listing all possible groups that have an interest in or are affected by the university's communications. Typical stakeholder groups for Indian universities include:

- **Current Students:** The primary audience for most university communications, encompassing undergraduates, postgraduates, and doctoral students.
- **Prospective Students:** High school students, transfer students, and international students considering your institution for their higher education.
- **Alumni:** Former students whose ongoing engagement and support are vital to the university's network and development.

- **Faculty and Staff:** Employees who need to stay informed about university policies, achievements, and opportunities.
- **Parents and Families:** Especially important for undergraduate students, as they often play a significant role in education decisions.
- **Research Partners and Industry Collaborators:** Entities involved in collaborative research, internships, placements, and other academic partnerships.
- **Government and Regulatory Bodies:** Departments and agencies that oversee higher education policies, funding, and accreditation.
- **Local Community:** Local residents and organizations that interact with or are impacted by the university.

Step 2: Segment Your Audience

After listing potential stakeholders, the next step is to segment these groups based on specific characteristics or interests. For example, prospective students can be segmented by field of interest, geographic location, or academic background. Segmentation allows for more personalized and relevant communications.

Step 3: Prioritize Your Audience

Not all audiences are equally critical to every communication effort. Prioritize your audiences based on the specific objectives of your communications plan. For instance, if the goal is to increase undergraduate enrollment, prospective students and their families might be the primary audience, with current students and alumni as secondary audiences to leverage for testimonials and word-of-mouth marketing.

Step 4: Understand Your Audience

Gather insights about your audiences' preferences, behaviors, and communication channels. This can involve:

- **Surveys and Feedback:** Collecting direct feedback from each group to understand their needs and preferences.
- **Data Analysis:** Utilizing enrollment data, social media analytics, and website traffic to identify trends and interests.
- **Persona Development:** Creating representative personas for each audience segment can help in visualizing their characteristics, challenges, and motivations.

Step 5: Tailor Your Communication Strategy

Using the insights gained from the steps above, tailor your communication messages, channels, and tactics to suit each audience segment.
For example:

- **Current and Prospective Students:** Utilize social media, email newsletters, and campus apps to share updates, success stories, and important deadlines.
- **Alumni:** Employ email campaigns, dedicated alumni networks, and special events to keep them engaged and encourage their support.
- **Faculty and Staff:** Internal newsletters, intranet portals, and regular meetings can ensure they are informed and involved.

Identifying and understanding your target audiences is a foundational step in any communications strategy. By taking a structured approach to audience identification, segmentation, and prioritization, Indian universities can ensure their communications are effective and capable of supporting institutional goals.

CHAPTER SIX

Crafting Your University's Brand Identity

Creating a strong and distinctive brand identity is essential for any university aiming to stand out in the competitive landscape of higher education. A well-defined brand identity not only communicates the university's values and strengths but also fosters a sense of pride and belonging among students, faculty, alumni, and other stakeholders. Here's how Indian universities can craft a compelling brand identity:

Define Your Core Values and Mission

Identify Core Values: What principles guide your institution? Integrity, innovation, inclusivity, and excellence are common values that can set the foundation for your brand.

Articulate Your Mission: Clearly define your university's mission. This should reflect your institution's purpose, aspirations, and the impact you seek to have on students and the wider community.

Establish a Unique Value Proposition

Highlight What Sets You Apart: Determine what differentiates your university from others. This could be specialized programs, a strong research focus, a vibrant campus culture, or notable alumni achievements.

Communicate Your Strengths: Ensure your unique offerings and strengths are front and center in your messaging.

Develop a Consistent Visual Identity

Logo and Color Scheme: Design a logo that reflects the essence of your university. Choose a color scheme that is visually appealing and reflects your institution's personality.

- **Typography and Imagery:** Select fonts and imagery that complement your visual identity and are consistent across all communications.

Craft a Compelling Narrative

Tell Your Story: Every university has a story to tell. Narrate your institution's history, achievements, and vision for the future in a way that resonates emotionally with your target audiences.

Use Authentic Voices: Incorporate testimonials from students, faculty, and alumni to add authenticity and depth to your brand narrative.

Ensure Consistency Across All Touchpoints

Develop Brand Guidelines: Create comprehensive brand guidelines that cover logo usage, color palette, typography, imagery, and tone of voice. This ensures consistency across all communications, from your website and social media to print materials and advertising.

Train Your Team: Ensure that everyone involved in communications understands and can effectively apply your brand guidelines.

Engage Your Community

Involve Stakeholders: Engage students, faculty, alumni, and other stakeholders in the branding process. Their insights and experiences can enrich your brand identity.

Live Your Brand: Beyond visual identity and messaging, ensure that your university's actions and experiences reflect your brand values. This includes everything from the quality of education and research to community engagement and campus culture.

Monitor and Evolve Your Brand Identity

Gather Feedback: Regularly solicit feedback from your community and target audiences to understand how your brand is perceived.

Stay Current: Be prepared to evolve your brand identity as your university grows and the landscape changes. Keeping your brand relevant and resonant is an ongoing process.

Crafting your university's brand identity is a strategic endeavor that requires thoughtful consideration of your unique values, strengths, and stories. By establishing a strong and cohesive brand, Indian universities can more effectively communicate their value proposition, engage their communities, and achieve their strategic goals.

CHAPTER SEVEN

Building Your Communications Team

Establishing a skilled and effective communications team is crucial for universities, especially in the dynamic and diverse landscape of Indian higher education. This team is responsible for managing the institution's messaging, enhancing its reputation, and engaging with various stakeholders. Here is a guide to assembling a team equipped to tackle these challenges successfully.

Define the Team's Structure and Roles

Assess Your Needs: Consider the scope of your communications strategy, including internal and external communications, digital marketing, public relations, crisis management, and alumni relations. This assessment will guide the size and specialization of your team.

Identify Key Roles: Common roles within a university communications team might include a Communications Director, Content Writers, Social Media Managers, PR Specialists, Graphic Designers, and Web Developers. Depending on your size and needs, these roles can be standalone positions or responsibilities shared among team members.

Look for Essential Skills and Qualities

Strong Writing and Storytelling Abilities: Essential for creating compelling content that resonates with your diverse audience.

Digital Savvy: Familiarity with digital marketing tools, social media platforms, and analytics is crucial in the digital age.

Strategic Thinking: Ability to develop and implement strategies that align with the university's goals and adapt to changing circumstances.

Crisis Management Skills: Competence in handling sensitive situations with tact and speed.

Teamwork and Collaboration: Given the interdisciplinary nature of communications, the ability to work collaboratively with other departments and stakeholders is vital.

Hiring and Training

Diverse Talent Pool: Aim to hire individuals with a range of backgrounds and experiences. Diversity in your team can lead to more creative and inclusive communications strategies.

Ongoing Professional Development: Offer opportunities for team members to stay updated on the latest communications tools, technologies, and best practices. Workshops, webinars, and conferences can be valuable resources.

Foster a Collaborative Culture

Encourage Open Communication: Regular meetings and open channels of communication can help ensure that everyone is aligned and that ideas and concerns are shared freely.

Recognize and Reward: Acknowledge individual and team achievements to motivate your team and reinforce the value of their work.

Leverage External Resources

Consultants and Freelancers: For specialized projects or to supplement your team's capabilities, consider hiring external experts. This can be particularly useful for tasks like website redesign, video production, or market research.

Collaborate with Academic Departments: Engage faculty and students in communications initiatives. They can offer valuable insights and contribute content that highlights academic excellence and innovation.

Use Technology to Enhance Efficiency

Project Management Tools: Utilize software like Asana, Trello, or Slack to manage projects, deadlines, and collaborations more effectively.

Content Management Systems: A robust CMS can streamline website updates and content publication, allowing your team to focus more on content creation and strategy.

Measure and Adapt

Set Clear Objectives and KPIs: Define what success looks like for your team, whether it's increasing engagement on social media, enhancing media coverage, or improving internal communications.

Regularly Review Performance: Use analytics and feedback to assess the impact of your communications efforts and identify areas for improvement.

Building a communications team is not a one-size-fits-all process. It requires thoughtful consideration of your university's unique needs, goals, and resources. By assembling a team with the right mix of skills, fostering a collaborative culture, and staying adaptable, Indian universities can enhance their communications effectiveness and achieve their strategic objectives.

Section 3 – Developing a Strategic Communications Plan

Steps to Create a Comprehensive Communications Plan

Creating a comprehensive communications plan is essential for universities to effectively share their message, engage with stakeholders, and achieve their strategic goals. A well-structured plan ensures that all communication efforts are aligned, targeted, and measurable. Here's a step-by-step guide tailored for Indian universities to develop an effective communications plan.

Step 1: Define Your Communications Objectives

Set Clear, Achievable Goals: Objectives should be specific, measurable, attainable, relevant, and time-bound (SMART). Whether it's increasing student enrollment, enhancing the university's reputation, or improving stakeholder engagement, your goals will guide all subsequent planning.

Step 2: Identify and Understand Your Target Audiences

Segment Audiences: Break down your larger audience into smaller, defined groups such as prospective students, current students, alumni, faculty, and industry partners. Understand their needs, preferences, and communication habits to tailor your messages effectively.

Step 3: Develop Key Messages

Craft Clear and Consistent Messages: Based on your objectives and audience insights, develop key messages that are compelling, relevant, and aligned with your university's brand identity. Ensure that these messages resonate with each target audience segment.

Step 4: Choose the Right Channels and Tools

Select Appropriate Channels: Determine the most effective channels for reaching each audience segment, considering a mix of traditional and digital media. This may include social media, email newsletters, press releases, and campus bulletins.

Leverage Communication Tools: Utilize tools such as content management systems, social media schedulers, and analytics platforms to streamline your communication efforts and measure success.

Step 5: Plan Your Content Strategy

Create a Content Calendar: Outline what content will be shared, when it will be shared, and through which channels. This calendar should align with key university dates, events, and initiatives.

Ensure Content Diversity: Plan for a variety of content types, such as news articles, blog posts, videos, and infographics, to keep your audience engaged and to convey your messages effectively.

Step 6: Assign Roles and Responsibilities

Define Team Roles: Clearly outline who is responsible for creating, approving, and distributing each type of content. Ensuring accountability will help keep your communications plan on track.

Foster Collaboration: Encourage coordination between departments and teams to ensure a cohesive and unified communication effort.

Step 7: Establish Budget and Resources

Allocate Budget: Identify the financial resources available for your communications activities, including external advertising, software subscriptions, and event hosting.

Resource Planning: Determine what human and technological resources are needed to execute your plan effectively.

Step 8: Implement the Plan

Execute Strategically: Begin rolling out your communications plan according to the established timeline and content calendar. Ensure all team members are aligned and aware of their roles in the implementation process.

Step 9: Monitor and Measure Impact

Set Key Performance Indicators (KPIs): Define clear metrics for success based on your initial objectives. These could include website traffic, social media engagement rates, or attendance at university events.

Regularly Review Analytics: Use tools to track the performance of your communications efforts and gather insights into what's working and what's not.

Step 10: Review and Adapt

Evaluate Success: Assess the effectiveness of your communications plan in achieving its objectives. Gather feedback from stakeholders to gain additional insights.

Iterate and Improve: Be prepared to make adjustments to your plan based on performance data and stakeholder feedback. Continuous improvement will help ensure your communications efforts remain effective and relevant.

Developing a comprehensive communications plan is a dynamic process that requires ongoing attention and adaptation. By following these steps, Indian universities can enhance their ability to communicate effectively with their diverse audiences, supporting their strategic goals and strengthening their community engagement.

CHAPTER NINE

Setting SMART Goals and Objectives

In the context of creating a communications plan for Indian universities, setting SMART (Specific, Measurable, Achievable, Relevant, Time-bound) goals and objectives is a fundamental step. This approach ensures clarity, focus, and accountability throughout the communications efforts, aligning them closely with the institution's overarching strategic goals. Here's how universities can set SMART goals and objectives for their communications plans.

Specific

Goals should be clear and specific to avoid ambiguity and focus efforts. Instead of a general goal like "increase awareness," a specific goal would be "increase awareness of the university's new sustainability initiative among students and faculty."

- **Who:** Identify the audience or stakeholders.
- **What:** Determine what needs to be accomplished.
- **Why:** Understand the importance of the goal.

Example: Increase prospective undergraduate student applications by 15% for the 2024 academic year by highlighting the success of recent graduates through targeted social media campaigns.

Measurable

A measurable goal includes precise criteria for tracking progress and determining success. This helps in keeping the team motivated and allows for adjustments to the strategy if needed.

- **How Much/Many:** Define quantifiable indicators of progress.
- **Tracking Tools:** Use analytics tools, surveys, and other methods to measure outcomes.

Example: Achieve a 25% increase in engagement (likes, shares, comments) on the university's official social media platforms within six months by sharing weekly success stories of alumni.

Achievable

Goals should be realistic, considering the resources, constraints, and external factors. Setting unattainable goals can demotivate your team and lead to resource wastage.

- **Resources and Capabilities:** Assess whether the university has the resources, or can obtain them, to achieve the goal.
- **Historical Data:** Look at past achievements to set attainable goals.

Example: Secure at least five media mentions for the university in national publications within the next quarter by pitching stories about innovative research conducted by faculty.

Relevant

Ensure the goals are aligned with the university's mission, values, and strategic objectives. Relevance ensures that the communications efforts contribute to the broader purpose and priorities of the institution.

- **Alignment with University Objectives:** Connect goals to the institution's strategic plan.
- **Stakeholder Value:** Goals should address the needs and interests of your target audiences.

Example: Enhance alumni engagement by 30% over the next year through targeted newsletters and exclusive networking events, supporting the university's objective of building a strong and supportive alumni network.

Time-bound

Setting a deadline provides a sense of urgency and helps prioritize tasks. It also facilitates the planning of resources and scheduling of related activities.

- **Deadline:** Specify when the result(s) should be achieved.
- **Milestones:** Break larger goals into smaller, time-specific milestones for better management.

Example: Increase website traffic by 20% in the next six months by optimizing web content for SEO and launching a monthly blog series featuring student and faculty achievements.

Implementing SMART Goals

After setting SMART goals, the next steps involve:

- **Action Planning:** Break down each goal into actionable steps.
- **Resource Allocation:** Ensure necessary resources are allocated to achieve each goal.
- **Monitoring and Adjustment:** Regularly monitor progress towards goals, ready to adjust strategies in response to feedback

and changing circumstances.

By setting SMART goals and objectives, Indian universities can create more focused, effective, and measurable communications plans that are aligned with their strategic vision and capable of achieving significant impact.

CHAPTER TEN

Audience Segmentation and Messaging

For universities, especially within the diverse context of Indian higher education, tailoring communications to meet the specific needs and preferences of different audience segments is crucial. Effective audience segmentation and targeted messaging ensure that the right messages reach the right people at the right time, enhancing engagement and achieving strategic communication goals. Here's how Indian universities can approach audience segmentation and craft compelling messages for each group.

Understanding Audience Segmentation

Audience segmentation involves dividing your broader audience into smaller, more homogeneous groups based on shared characteristics or behaviors. This allows for more personalized and relevant communications.

Criteria for Segmentation:

- **Demographic Factors:** Age, gender, educational background, geographic location.

- **Psychographic Factors:** Interests, attitudes, values, and lifestyle.

- **Behavioral Factors:** Engagement with the university's communication channels, participation in university events, and response to past communications.

- **Needs and Preferences:** Specific information needs, communication preferences, and concerns or challenges faced by the audience.

Developing Targeted Messaging

Once you've identified your segments, the next step is to develop messages tailored to the interests, needs, and behaviors of each group. This ensures that your communications are relevant and engaging.

Crafting Messages:

- **Align with Audience Needs and Values:** Messages should speak directly to what is important to each audience segment, whether it's career advancement for alumni, research opportunities for faculty, or campus life for prospective students.

- **Use the Appropriate Tone and Language:** The tone should resonate with the audience segment. For example, communications with prospective students might be more informal and energetic, while messages to government bodies might be more formal and data-driven.

- **Highlight Benefits and Solutions:** Focus on how your university addresses the specific needs or interests of the audience segment, such as detailing scholarship opportunities for financially needy students or spotlighting faculty research grants.

Examples of Audience Segmentation and Messaging

1. Prospective Students

- **Segmentation Criteria:** Academic interests, location, and stage in the application process.

- **Messaging:** Highlight unique academic programs, success stories of recent graduates, and campus life through personalized emails and social media campaigns.

2. Current Students

- **Segmentation Criteria:** Year of study, department, and extracurricular interests.

- **Messaging:** Share relevant academic resources, upcoming events, and support services through targeted newsletters and a student app.

3. Alumni

- **Segmentation Criteria:** Graduation year, industry, and level of prior engagement with the university.

- **Messaging:** Foster a sense of ongoing community through alumni success stories, networking event invitations, and opportunities to mentor current students, using segmented email campaigns and exclusive online platforms.

4. Faculty and Staff

- **Segmentation Criteria:** Department, role, and tenure at the university.

- **Messaging:** Communicate important administrative updates, professional development opportunities, and departmental achievements through internal newsletters and intranet announcements.

Implementing Segmented Communications

- **Use the Right Channels:** Choose communication channels preferred by each segment, whether it's social media, email, webinars, or traditional mail.

- **Test and Learn:** Experiment with different messages and formats to see what resonates best with each segment, using A/B testing where possible.

- **Measure and Adjust:** Monitor engagement metrics and gather feedback to refine your segmentation and messaging strategy over time.

By effectively segmenting their audience and tailoring their messaging, Indian universities can improve the impact of their communications, enhancing engagement, satisfaction, and loyalty among all stakeholders.

CHAPTER ELEVEN

Channel Strategy: Choosing the Right Platforms

For Indian universities, developing a strategic approach to choosing communication channels is pivotal in effectively reaching and engaging with their diverse audiences. The landscape of communication channels has expanded significantly, encompassing traditional media, digital platforms, and emerging technologies. Selecting the right mix of these channels ensures that your messages resonate with your target audiences, fostering better connections and achieving your communication goals.

Understanding Your Audience

Before selecting channels, it's essential to have a deep understanding of your target audiences, including their preferences, behaviors, and the platforms they frequent. For instance, prospective students might be more active on social media platforms like Instagram and YouTube, while alumni may prefer LinkedIn or email newsletters for updates and engagement.

Evaluating Channel Options

1. Digital Platforms

- **Social Media:** Platforms like Instagram, Facebook, Twitter, LinkedIn, and YouTube are excellent for reaching a broad audience, including prospective and current students, alumni, and industry partners. Each platform serves different content preferences, from short updates on Twitter to in-depth videos on YouTube.

- **Email:** Highly effective for personalized communication with specific segments like prospective students, current students, alumni, and donors. Email newsletters can keep these groups informed about university news, events, and opportunities.

- **University Website:** The cornerstone of your digital presence, useful for providing comprehensive information about academic programs, admissions, research, campus life, and news.

2. Traditional Media

- Press Releases and Media Outreach: Essential for sharing significant university achievements, research breakthroughs, and events with a wider audience through newspapers, television, and radio.
   - Print Materials: Brochures, flyers, and posters remain effective for specific purposes, such as campus tours, recruitment fairs, and informational mailers to prospective students and their families.

3. Emerging Technologies

- **Mobile Apps:** Custom university apps can enhance the student experience by providing easy access to resources, services, and campus communities.

- **Podcasts and Webinars:** Growing in popularity, these platforms are great for showcasing faculty expertise, research findings, and discussing topical issues affecting the higher education sector.

Crafting a Multi-Channel Strategy

- **Integrated Approach:** Ensure your messaging is consistent across all channels while tailoring the content to fit the platform's unique format and audience.

- **Prioritize Based on Objectives:** Align your channel selection with your specific communication objectives. For example, if the goal is to increase prospective student engagement, prioritize social media and virtual tours on your website.

- **Resource Allocation:** Consider your resources, including budget, staff expertise, and time. Focus on channels that offer the best ROI in terms of your objectives.

Monitoring and Adjusting Your Strategy

- **Analytics and Feedback:** Use data analytics tools available on most digital platforms to monitor engagement and reach. Collect feedback from your target audiences to understand their preferences and experiences.

- **Flexibility:** The digital landscape is constantly evolving. Be prepared to adapt your strategy, experimenting with new channels and technologies as they emerge and as audience behaviors change.

Choosing the right communication channels is a dynamic process that requires a deep understanding of your audience, strategic planning, and ongoing evaluation. By effectively leveraging a mix of digital platforms, traditional media, and emerging technologies, Indian universities can enhance their visibility, engage with their stakeholders more effectively, and achieve their communication and engagement goals.

Section 4 - Digital Communications Strategy

CHAPTER TWELVE

Website Management and Optimization for Indian Universities

A university's website serves as a central hub for information, resources, and engagement for current and prospective students, faculty, staff, alumni, and other stakeholders. For Indian universities, where the diversity and volume of visitors can be particularly high, managing and optimizing the website is crucial to ensure accessibility, relevance, and user satisfaction. Here's a comprehensive approach to effective website management and optimization.

Website Structure and Navigation

User-Centric Design: Structure your website with the user in mind. Navigation should be intuitive, allowing visitors to find information quickly and easily. Use clear categories and a logical hierarchy.

Accessibility: Ensure your website is accessible to all users, including those with disabilities. This means adhering to WCAG (Web Content Accessibility Guidelines) by providing text alternatives for non-text content, making it navigable through keyboard only, etc.

Content Management

Relevant and Updated Content: Keep your content current to reflect the latest academic programs, events, and university news. Regular updates encourage repeat visits and improve your site's SEO.

Multimedia Elements: Incorporate videos, images, and infographics to make content more engaging. Ensure multimedia is optimized for fast loading times and is accessible.

Language and Tone: Use language that resonates with your diverse audience, keeping it professional yet approachable. Including content in multiple languages can also enhance accessibility and engagement, particularly in linguistically diverse India.

Search Engine Optimization (SEO)

Keyword Research: Identify keywords that prospective students, researchers, and faculty might use to find information related to your university. Incorporate these keywords naturally into your content.

Mobile Optimization: With the increasing use of smartphones, ensure your website is mobile-friendly. This affects both user experience and search engine rankings.

Loading Speed: Optimize website elements to ensure fast loading times. Slow websites can deter visitors and negatively impact your SEO.

Security and Privacy

SSL Certificate: Secure your website with an SSL certificate to protect users' information. This is crucial for any forms or portals that collect personal data.

Privacy Policy: Clearly state your privacy policy and adhere to data protection regulations, informing users how their data will be used and protected.

Analytics and Feedback

Use Analytics: Implement web analytics to track visitor behavior, including most visited pages, bounce rates, and visitor demographics. This data is invaluable for ongoing optimization efforts.

Gather User Feedback: Regularly solicit feedback from your website users through surveys or feedback forms. This direct input can guide improvements and enhancements.

Engagement and Interactivity

Contact and Support Options: Provide clear contact information and consider live chat or chatbot services for instant support. FAQ sections can also address common queries efficiently.

Social Media Integration: Integrate your social media channels to encourage further engagement. Shareable content can also increase your university's visibility online.

Training and Governance

Staff Training: Ensure that staff managing the website are trained in best practices for web design, content management, SEO, and accessibility.

• 54 •

Content Governance: Establish a governance model for content creation, approval, and publishing to maintain high quality and consistency.

By focusing on these key areas of website management and optimization, Indian universities can significantly enhance their online presence. A well-managed and optimized website not only serves as a valuable resource for its audiences but also as a powerful tool for achieving the institution's broader communication and engagement goals.

CHAPTER THIRTEEN

Social Media Strategy for Engagement and Growth

In the context of Indian universities, developing a robust social media strategy is pivotal for enhancing engagement with students, alumni, and prospective students, as well as for fostering a sense of community and belonging. The landscape of social media offers a dynamic platform for storytelling, sharing successes, and interactive communication. Here's how Indian universities can craft a social media strategy that promotes engagement and growth.

Define Your Objectives

Start by establishing clear, measurable goals for what you want to achieve through social media. These could range from increasing awareness of university programs, boosting engagement with current and prospective students, to fostering alumni relationships. Setting specific objectives will guide your content strategy and help in measuring success.

Know Your Audience

Understanding your audience is crucial to tailor your content and choose the right platforms. Indian universities have a diverse audience, including current students, prospective students (both domestic and international), alumni, faculty, and parents.

Segmenting these audiences and understanding their preferences and behaviors on social media will enable more targeted and effective communication.

Choose the Right Platforms

Not all social media platforms are equal, especially when considering the varied demographics and interests of your audience. Focus on platforms where your target audiences are most active. For Indian universities, this might include:

- **Facebook and Instagram:** Popular for engaging current and prospective students with visual content, stories, and campus updates.

- **LinkedIn:** Ideal for professional networking, showcasing alumni success stories, and highlighting faculty research and achievements.

- **Twitter:** Useful for real-time updates, news sharing, and engaging in broader conversations within the education sector.

- **YouTube:** For sharing video content such as virtual tours, lectures, and student testimonials.

Content Strategy

- **Diverse and Relevant Content:** Your content should reflect the diversity and vibrancy of campus life. Include academic achievements, student and faculty stories, event highlights, and informative content about admissions and programs.

- **Interactive Content:** Leverage polls, quizzes, and Q&A sessions to foster interaction. Live sessions and webinars can also engage audiences in real-time.

- **User-Generated Content:** Encourage students, alumni, and faculty to share their experiences and stories. This not only provides authentic content but also fosters a strong community feeling.

Consistency and Scheduling

Maintaining a consistent posting schedule is key to keeping your audience engaged and ensuring your social media channels remain active and relevant. Use scheduling tools to plan your posts and maintain a steady flow of content.

Engagement and Community Building

Engagement is a two-way street. Respond to comments, messages, and mentions in a timely manner to foster a sense of community and show that your institution values its audience. Highlighting user-generated content and participating in relevant online conversations can also strengthen community ties.

Monitoring and Analytics

Use social media analytics tools to track the performance of your content, understand audience behavior, and refine your strategy over time. Key metrics to focus on include engagement rates, follower growth, and the effectiveness of different types of content.

Adapting and Evolving

The social media landscape is constantly changing, with new trends, features, and audience preferences emerging regularly. Stay adaptable and open to experimenting with new ideas and platforms to keep your strategy fresh and effective.

By implementing these strategies, Indian universities can leverage social media to enhance their brand presence, engage with key stakeholders, and create a vibrant online community that reflects the dynamic spirit of their campuses.

CHAPTER FOURTEEN

Email Marketing: Best Practices for Universities

Email marketing remains a powerful tool for universities, offering a direct line of communication to current and prospective students, alumni, faculty, and other stakeholders. It allows for personalized, targeted communication that can significantly enhance engagement and support strategic objectives. For Indian universities, where the audience is diverse and the competition for attention is high, adhering to best practices in email marketing is crucial. Here are key strategies to ensure your email marketing efforts are effective and impactful.

1. Build a Clean, Segmented Email List

Voluntary Subscriptions: Ensure your email list comprises individuals who have opted in to receive communications from you. This not only complies with data protection laws but also improves engagement rates.

Segmentation: Segment your email list based on relevant criteria such as academic interest, enrollment status (prospective, current, or alumni), and engagement level. This enables more personalized and relevant communications.

2. Personalize Your Emails

Tailor the Content: Use the recipient's name and tailor the email content based on the segment to which they belong. Personalized emails tend to have higher open and engagement rates.

Dynamic Content: Utilize dynamic content that changes based on the recipient's preferences or past behavior to make emails even more relevant and engaging.

3. Craft Compelling Subject Lines

Clear and Concise: Keep your subject lines short, clear, and to the point. A well-crafted subject line can significantly increase the chances of your email being opened.

Invoke Curiosity: Use subject lines that pique interest but avoid clickbait tactics that might disappoint readers once they open the email.

4. Design for Readability and Accessibility

Mobile Optimization: Ensure your emails are mobile-friendly, as a significant portion of users access their emails via mobile devices.

Visual Appeal: Use a clean, visually appealing layout with well-spaced content and branded elements. Include images or videos to enhance engagement, but make sure the email is still accessible to those who might disable images.

Accessibility: Use alt text for images and ensure your email content is accessible to recipients with disabilities.

5. Provide Clear Calls to Action

Clarity in Action: Make it clear what action you want the recipient to take, whether it's applying for a program, registering for an event, or reading a news article.

Button Over Links: Use buttons for your calls to action (CTAs) instead of hyperlinks, as they are more visible and mobile-friendly.

6. Monitor and Optimize Based on Metrics

Key Performance Indicators (KPIs): Track open rates, click-through rates, conversion rates, and unsubscribe rates to gauge the effectiveness of your email campaigns.

A/B Testing: Regularly test different elements of your emails (such as subject lines, email content, and CTAs) to see what works best and continuously optimize your strategy based on data.

7. Respect Privacy and Compliance

Compliance with Regulations: Adhere to email marketing laws and regulations, including the General Data Protection Regulation (GDPR) for European recipients and similar regulations in other jurisdictions.

Unsubscribe Options: Always include an easy-to-find unsubscribe link in your emails, allowing recipients to opt out of future communications if they wish.

8. Leverage Automation and Drip Campaigns

Automated Welcome Series: Set up automated emails for new subscribers, providing them with a warm welcome and introducing them to what they can expect from your communications.

Drip Campaigns: Utilize drip campaigns for prospective students, guiding them through the application process or keeping them engaged with relevant content leading up to enrollment decisions.

Implementing these best practices can significantly enhance the effectiveness of email marketing campaigns for Indian universities. By communicating in a personalized, respectful, and engaging manner, universities can strengthen their relationships with their communities, support their strategic goals, and stand out in a crowded educational landscape.

Content Marketing for Higher Education

Content marketing in the higher education sector involves creating and sharing valuable, relevant, and consistent content to attract and retain a clearly defined audience — ultimately, to drive profitable customer action. For Indian universities, this strategy not only helps in engaging prospective and current students but also strengthens relationships with alumni, faculty, and potential collaborators. Here's how to effectively leverage content marketing within the higher education landscape.

Define Your Content Marketing Goals

Increase Enrollment: Use content to highlight unique programs, faculty excellence, and student success stories to attract prospective students.

Boost Brand Awareness: Share insights and innovations that position your university as a thought leader in key research areas.

Engage Current Students and Alumni: Create content that fosters a strong sense of community and keeps students and alumni connected to the university.

Know Your Audience

Segment Your Audience: Understand the needs, interests, and challenges of your diverse stakeholders, including prospective students, current students, alumni, faculty, and industry partners.

Persona Development: Create detailed personas for each segment to guide the tone, style, and subjects of your content.

Develop a Content Strategy

Content Calendar: Plan your content in advance, aligning with academic cycles, admission dates, and significant events.

Content Mix: Use a variety of formats such as blog posts, videos, infographics, podcasts, and social media posts to engage different segments of your audience.

Storytelling: Tell compelling stories that resonate emotionally with your audience, such as student achievements, research breakthroughs, and campus life experiences.

Optimize for Search Engines (SEO)

Keyword Research: Identify keywords that your target audience uses to find information related to your offerings.

SEO Best Practices: Optimize your content for search engines by incorporating keywords naturally, using meta tags, and creating quality backlinks.

Leverage Social Media

Share and Promote Content: Use your university's social media channels to share and promote your content, reaching a wider audience.

Engage with Your Community: Encourage comments, shares, and discussions around your content to increase engagement.

Measure and Analyze Performance

Set Key Performance Indicators (KPIs): Track metrics such as website traffic, engagement rates, lead generation, and conversion rates to gauge the effectiveness of your content marketing strategy.

Adjust Based on Insights: Regularly review performance data and use these insights to refine your content strategy, topics, and distribution channels.

Examples of Effective Content Marketing in Higher Education

Blog Series on Research Impact: Showcase how research conducted at your university is making a difference in the world.

Student and Alumni Success Stories: Feature stories of notable achievements by current students and alumni to inspire prospective students and foster a sense of pride among current students and alumni.

Faculty Spotlights: Highlight the expertise and accomplishments of your faculty to attract prospective students and research collaborators.

Virtual Campus Tours: Offer immersive virtual tours of your campus to prospective students who can't visit in person, using videos or VR technology.

Webinars and Online Workshops: Provide value to prospective and current students with free, informative sessions on topics related to academic success, career planning, and personal development.

Content marketing for higher education is not just about promoting a university's programs and achievements; it's about creating a dialogue and building relationships with your audience. By providing valuable, relevant content, Indian universities can engage their diverse stakeholders in meaningful ways, supporting their goals of enrollment growth, community engagement, and enhanced brand visibility.

Leveraging SEO for Increased Visibility

Search Engine Optimization (SEO) is a critical component of digital marketing strategies for Indian universities, aiming to improve their online visibility and attract more prospective students, faculty, and researchers. By optimizing their websites and content for search engines, universities can ensure that their programs, research opportunities, and campus amenities are easily discoverable by those seeking information online. Here's how institutions can leverage SEO to enhance their visibility.

Conduct Comprehensive Keyword Research

Identify Relevant Keywords: Use tools like Google Keyword Planner, SEMrush, or Ahrefs to find keywords related to the courses, programs, and research opportunities offered by your university. Include long-tail keywords which are more specific and less competitive.

Understand User Intent: Classify keywords based on user intent — informational (looking for information), navigational (looking for a specific page), and transactional (ready to apply or inquire). Tailor your content to match these intents.

Optimize Website Structure and Navigation

User-Friendly Design: Ensure your website is easy to navigate, with a clear hierarchy and logical structure. A well-organized site helps search engines index your pages more effectively.

Mobile Optimization: With the majority of searches now performed on mobile devices, having a mobile-responsive website is crucial for both user experience and search ranking.

Fast Loading Speed: Page speed is a ranking factor for search engines. Optimize images, minify code, and leverage browser caching to improve loading times.

Create High-Quality, Relevant Content

Content is King: Develop engaging, informative content that addresses the needs and interests of your target audience. This can include blog posts, research summaries, faculty interviews, and student testimonials.

Use Keywords Strategically: Incorporate keywords naturally into your content, titles, headings, and meta descriptions. Avoid keyword stuffing, which can penalize your site.

Update Regularly: Keep your content fresh and updated. Regularly publishing new content not only provides value to your audience but also signals to search engines that your site is active and relevant.

Build Quality Backlinks

Authority and Credibility: Backlinks from reputable sites enhance your site's authority and can significantly improve your search ranking. Strive to get your university's research, events, and academic programs featured or mentioned in reputable educational and news websites.

Collaborate with Academia and Industry: Encourage faculty and students to contribute to external publications and websites, linking back to your university's site.

Utilize Local SEO

Google My Business: For universities looking to attract students locally or nationally, setting up a Google My Business profile can improve local search visibility. Include detailed information such as location, contact details, and campus opening hours.

Local Keywords: Incorporate location-based keywords into your website and content to attract students looking for universities in specific areas.

Monitor and Analyze Your SEO Efforts

Use Analytics: Tools like Google Analytics and Google Search Console can provide insights into your website's performance, visitor behavior, and how users are finding your site.

Continuous Improvement: SEO is not a one-time task but an ongoing process. Regularly review your analytics, stay updated on SEO best practices, and adjust your strategies accordingly.

By implementing these SEO strategies, Indian universities can improve their online visibility, making it easier for prospective students, faculty, and partners to discover what they offer. Effective SEO not only enhances the institution's digital presence but also supports broader marketing and recruitment goals.

Section 5 – Public Relations and Media Outreach

CHAPTER SEVENTEEN

Crafting Effective Press Releases

In the dynamic landscape of higher education, press releases are a valuable tool for Indian universities to announce significant developments, achievements, and events. A well-crafted press release can capture the media's attention, enhance the institution's visibility, and communicate key messages to a broader audience. Here's a guide to creating effective press releases that stand out.

Define Your Objective

Clear Purpose: Before writing, clearly define the purpose of your press release. Whether it's announcing a new program, research breakthrough, upcoming event, or a significant achievement, the objective should guide the content and tone.

Craft a Compelling Headline

Attention-Grabbing: The headline is your first opportunity to capture interest. Make it compelling and informative, ensuring it reflects the core news angle of your release.

Clarity: While creativity is important, clarity should not be sacrificed. The headline should give a clear indication of the press release's content.

Write a Strong Opening Paragraph

The 5 Ws: Your opening paragraph should answer the 5 Ws - Who, What, When, Where, Why (and How, if applicable). This ensures that even if only the first paragraph is read, the essential information is communicated.

Conciseness: Be concise yet informative, providing the most critical details upfront to hook the reader's interest.

Provide Detailed Information

Body Paragraphs: Following the introduction, delve into more detail about the news. Include quotes from relevant university representatives (e.g., Chancellor, Dean, or Program Director) to add credibility and a personal touch.

Data and Statistics: Where applicable, include data or statistics to substantiate your claims and add weight to the announcement.

Include Quotes

Authority and Perspective: Quotes from university leaders, faculty members, or involved parties add authority to your press release and provide insights into the significance of the announcement.

Human Element: A well-chosen quote can also add a human element, making your press release more engaging and relatable.

Add a Clear Call to Action (CTA)

Next Steps: Guide the reader on what to do next — whether it's visiting a website for more information, attending an event, or how to get in touch for further inquiries.

Accessibility: Ensure that the CTA is clear and that any links or contact information provided are accurate and easily accessible.

Include Essential and Optional Elements

Boilerplate: End with a boilerplate statement about the university, offering a brief overview of its history, mission, and key achievements.

Media Contact Information: Provide the name, phone number, and email address of the university's media contact person. This is crucial for journalists who may have follow-up questions or need additional information.

Multimedia Elements: Whenever possible, include or offer links to high-quality photos, videos, or infographics related to the announcement. Visual elements can significantly increase the chances of your press release getting noticed and shared.

Follow Press Release Formatting Guidelines

Professional Format: Use a standard press release format, with clear section headings and an easy-to-read font. Keep it to one page if possible, or two pages maximum.

Proofread and Edit: Ensure the press release is free of grammatical errors and typos, as these can detract from its credibility.

Timing and Distribution

Timing: Consider the timing of your release to maximize impact. Avoid releasing it during times when it might be overshadowed by bigger news events.

Distribution: Use both traditional (newspapers, television) and digital (social media, online news portals) channels for distribution, targeting those most relevant to your audience.

Crafting effective press releases requires attention to detail, a clear understanding of your audience, and an ability to highlight the newsworthiness of your announcement. By following these guidelines, Indian universities can enhance the impact of their press releases and achieve greater visibility for their accomplishments and initiatives.

CHAPTER EIGHTEEN

Media Relations: Building Productive Relationships with Journalists

For Indian universities, fostering positive relationships with journalists is essential for enhancing media coverage and public perception. Effective media relations not only help in disseminating university news and achievements but also in managing the institution's reputation during crises. Here's how universities can build and maintain productive relationships with journalists.

Understand the Media Landscape

Research: Familiarize yourself with the media outlets and journalists who cover education and related topics. Understand their interests, beats, and the types of stories they typically cover.

Media List: Create a media list that includes key contacts relevant to your university's activities and achievements. Regularly update this list to keep track of journalist movements and preferences.

Establish Initial Contact

Personalized Approach: When reaching out for the first time, personalize your communication. Mention specific articles they've written that align with your university's activities to show that you've done your homework.

Provide Value: Offer exclusive insights, data, or access to experts that can help journalists in their reporting. Making their job easier can start the relationship on the right foot.

Be a Reliable Source

Timeliness: Respond promptly to media inquiries, even if it's just to say you're working on getting the information. Journalists often work on tight deadlines, and being responsive can make you a go-to source.

Accuracy: Ensure that all information provided to journalists is accurate and well-researched. Building a reputation for reliability is crucial.

Offer Exclusive Opportunities

Exclusive Content: Offer exclusive stories or interviews to journalists who have shown a keen interest in your university. This can lead to deeper, more meaningful coverage.

Access to Events: Invite journalists to campus events, press conferences, and briefings. Personal interactions can strengthen relationships and lead to better engagement.

Provide Useful Resources

Press Kit: Prepare an electronic press kit that includes high-resolution images, bios of key faculty and administrators, recent press releases, and fast facts about the university. Make it easily accessible on your university's website.

Expert Database: Create a list of faculty experts willing to speak with the media on various topics. This can be invaluable for journalists looking for expert commentary or analysis.

Engage on Social Media

Follow and Interact: Follow relevant journalists and media outlets on social media. Engage with their content in a meaningful way to increase visibility and foster connection.

Share Their Work: When journalists cover your university, share the content across your social media platforms and website. Acknowledging their work can foster goodwill.

Train Your Spokespeople

Media Training: Provide media training for university spokespeople, including how to handle difficult questions and stay on message. Being well-prepared can lead to more positive interactions with the press.

Accessibility: Make sure journalists have easy access to your spokespeople when needed, especially during critical news cycles.

Feedback and Appreciation

Constructive Feedback: If there are inaccuracies in a story, provide feedback constructively and politely. Maintaining a professional demeanor is key.

Show Appreciation: Thank journalists for fair and comprehensive coverage. A simple thank you can go a long way in maintaining a positive relationship.

• 80 •

Building productive relationships with journalists requires ongoing effort, transparency, and a commitment to providing value. For Indian universities, these relationships are not just about securing more coverage but about creating partnerships that can enhance public understanding and support for their educational missions and achievements.

CHAPTER NINETEEN

Handling Negative Publicity and Crisis Communication

Universities, like any large organization, can sometimes face situations that may lead to negative publicity. These can range from minor issues that attract media attention to more significant crises that threaten the institution's reputation. Effective crisis communication is essential in these situations, allowing universities to manage their response and mitigate potential damage. Here's a guide for Indian universities on handling negative publicity and mastering crisis communication.

Pre-Crisis Planning

Crisis Communication Plan: Develop a comprehensive crisis communication plan that outlines procedures for various scenarios. This plan should include a crisis response team, key spokespersons, and a list of stakeholders.

Training and Simulations: Regularly train your crisis response team and conduct simulations to ensure everyone is prepared to act swiftly and effectively in a real crisis.

During a Crisis

Quick and Coordinated Response: Time is of the essence. Coordinate with your crisis communication team to assess the situation and decide on immediate actions.

Centralized Information Control: Designate a single source of information (such as a spokesperson or a dedicated webpage) to avoid conflicting messages and ensure consistency in communication.

Transparency and Honesty: Be as open and transparent as possible with what you know, what you don't know, and what you're doing about the situation. Honesty builds trust, even in difficult circumstances.

Communicating with Stakeholders

Immediate Notification: Inform all internal stakeholders (faculty, staff, students) about the situation before they learn about it through external sources. Use direct communication channels like email or intranet announcements.

Regular Updates: Keep all stakeholders updated as the situation evolves. Regular, scheduled updates can help manage expectations and reduce uncertainty.

Empathetic Tone: Use a tone that is empathetic and understanding of the concerns and emotions of those affected by the crisis.

Engaging with the Media

Prepare Statements: Have prepared statements that can be quickly adapted to the specific details of the crisis. These should convey the university's concern and commitment to addressing the issue.

Media Briefings: If necessary, hold media briefings to address the crisis publicly. Ensure your spokesperson is well-prepared and capable of handling tough questions.

Monitor Media Coverage: Keep a close eye on how the crisis is being reported and be ready to correct any inaccuracies or provide additional information as needed.

Post-Crisis Evaluation

Review and Reflect: After the crisis has been resolved, conduct a thorough review of how it was handled. What worked well? What could have been done differently? This reflection is crucial for improving future responses.

Repair and Rebuild: Take steps to repair any damage to relationships with stakeholders and to rebuild trust. This might include outreach programs, community engagement initiatives, or policy changes based on lessons learned.

Leveraging Digital Media

Social Media Monitoring: Use social media monitoring tools to keep track of the conversation around the crisis. Responding appropriately on these platforms can be a vital part of your strategy.

Online Updates: Use your university's website and social media channels to provide updates and counter misinformation.

Legal Considerations

Legal Counsel: Consult with legal counsel to understand any potential legal implications of the crisis and to ensure that communications are compliant with legal requirements.

Handling negative publicity and managing crisis communication effectively require careful planning, rapid response, and a commitment to transparency and integrity. By following these guidelines, Indian universities can navigate challenging situations more effectively, minimizing damage and maintaining trust with their stakeholders.

CHAPTER TWENTY

Organizing Successful Press Conferences

Press conferences are a strategic tool for Indian universities to communicate important announcements, achievements, or to address significant issues directly with the media. When organized effectively, they can enhance the institution's visibility, shape public perception, and provide an opportunity for real-time interaction with the press. Here's a guide to organizing successful press conferences in the context of Indian universities.

Pre-Event Planning

Define the Purpose: Clearly identify the reason for the press conference. Whether it's announcing a new research breakthrough, launching a new program, or addressing a crisis, the purpose will guide the planning process.

Select the Right Time and Venue: Choose a time that does not clash with major news events or other industry press conferences. The venue should be easily accessible for journalists, with adequate facilities for broadcasting and recording.

Prepare Press Kits: Assemble press kits containing detailed information about the announcement, including press releases, backgrounders, biographies of spokespersons, and high-quality images or graphics. Digital press kits are increasingly preferred for their convenience and accessibility.

Invite the Media

Targeted Invitations: Send personalized invitations to journalists, editors, and media outlets that cover higher education or related fields. Include bloggers and online media influencers if relevant to your audience.

Follow-Up: A few days before the event, follow up with those who have not responded to confirm attendance. This is also a good time to answer any preliminary questions they might have.

Speaker Preparation

Select Key Spokespersons: Choose speakers who are not only knowledgeable about the subject matter but are also comfortable speaking in public and handling difficult questions from the press.

Rehearse: Conduct a rehearsal with all speakers to review their speeches or presentations, anticipate possible questions from the media, and practice concise and clear responses.

On the Day of the Press Conference

Early Setup: Arrive early to check the setup, ensuring that the venue is arranged as planned, with all necessary equipment in place and working properly.

Registration Desk: Set up a registration desk at the entrance to greet journalists, hand out press kits, and provide badges or identification if necessary.

Technical Check: Ensure that all technical aspects, such as microphones, projectors, and internet connections, are functioning correctly. Have technical support on standby for any last-minute issues.

Conducting the Press Conference

Start on Time: Begin the press conference at the scheduled time as a courtesy to attendees.

Clear and Concise Presentations: Speakers should deliver their messages clearly and concisely, sticking to the key points and avoiding jargon.

Q&A Session: Allocate ample time for questions and answers, encouraging an open and constructive dialogue with the media. Speakers should remain calm, respectful, and professional, even when faced with tough questions.

Post-Press Conference

Distribute Press Releases: Immediately after the press conference, distribute the press release to all attendees and to your wider media list. This ensures that the information is available for those who could not attend.

Media Monitoring: Monitor media coverage following the press conference to assess its impact and gather insights for future events.

Thank You Notes: Send thank you notes to journalists who attended, offering to provide additional information or arrange follow-up interviews as needed.

Organizing a successful press conference requires meticulous planning, attention to detail, and effective communication, both in the preparation phase and during the event itself. By following these guidelines, Indian universities can maximize the impact of their press conferences, ensuring their messages are heard and accurately reported.

Section 6 – Internal Communications

CHAPTER TWENTY-ONE

Importance of Internal Communications in Universities

In the complex ecosystem of a university, where diverse groups coalesce around the shared goals of education, research, and community engagement, the role of internal communications becomes pivotal. Effective internal communications within universities, especially in the culturally rich and diverse context of India, ensure that faculty, staff, and students are informed, engaged, and aligned with the institution's values and objectives. Here's why internal communications are so vital:

Enhancing Community Engagement

Building a Unified Culture: Effective internal communications foster a sense of belonging and community among all members of the university. They help in building a unified culture that values diversity, inclusion, and mutual respect.

Facilitating Collaboration: By promoting open lines of communication, universities can encourage collaboration across departments and disciplines, leading to innovative research and interdisciplinary learning opportunities.

Supporting Change Management

Navigating Change: Universities today face rapid changes—be it in technology, educational policies, or global partnerships. Clear and consistent internal communications support the effective management of change, reducing uncertainty and resistance among the university community.

Promoting Adaptability: Regular updates and transparent communication about ongoing changes prepare the university community to adapt quickly, ensuring the institution remains competitive and responsive to external pressures.

Improving Academic Performance

Aligning Goals: Clearly communicated academic goals and standards help align the efforts of faculty and students, promoting a more focused and productive learning environment.

Enhancing Learning Experience: Effective communication channels allow for feedback loops between students and faculty, which can significantly enhance the learning experience and academic outcomes.

Boosting Morale and Satisfaction

Recognition and Achievement: Internal communications platforms can be used to celebrate achievements, recognize individual or team contributions, and highlight stories of excellence within the university. This not only boosts morale but also motivates others towards high performance.

Addressing Concerns: Providing a forum for voicing concerns or suggestions and ensuring those are addressed, contributes to a more satisfied university community, where members feel valued and heard.

Facilitating Crisis Communication

Preparedness and Response: In times of crisis, having established channels for internal communication ensures that accurate information can be disseminated quickly, minimizing rumors and misinformation.

Recovery and Support: Post-crisis, internal communications play a crucial role in the recovery process, offering support resources, counseling services, and updates on return-to-normalcy plans.

Streamlining Administrative Processes

Efficiency in Operations: Clear directives and updates on administrative processes, policy changes, and procedural updates through internal communications can significantly enhance operational efficiency.

Transparency in Decision-Making: Communicating the rationale behind decisions, especially those that directly affect faculty and students, can foster an environment of transparency and trust.

Strategies for Effective Internal Communications

Diverse Channels: Utilize a mix of communication channels—emails, intranet, newsletters, and meetings—to reach different segments of the university population effectively.

Feedback Mechanisms: Implement channels for feedback, allowing community members to voice opinions, concerns, and suggestions. This not only improves engagement but also provides valuable insights for university leadership.

Regular Updates: Maintain a schedule of regular communications to keep the community informed about developments, changes, and events within the university.

In summary, effective internal communications are foundational to building a cohesive, informed, and engaged university community. For Indian universities, navigating the diverse linguistic, cultural, and disciplinary landscapes, these communications are indispensable in achieving institutional harmony and advancing collective goals.

CHAPTER TWENTY-TWO

Tools and Techniques for Effective Internal Communications

Effective internal communications within a university can significantly enhance collaboration, morale, and the overall educational experience. With the diversity and size of universities, especially in a multifaceted educational landscape like India's, employing a range of tools and techniques is crucial for reaching and engaging all members of the campus community. Here's a look at some effective tools and techniques that can aid in streamlining internal communications.

Digital Communication Platforms

Email: While ubiquitous, email remains a primary tool for official communications, important announcements, and distributing newsletters or bulletins.

Intranet: A well-designed intranet can serve as a central hub for news, resources, administrative documents, and more, accessible to faculty, staff, and students.

Collaboration Tools: Platforms like Microsoft Teams, Slack, or

Google Workspace facilitate real-time collaboration, instant messaging, and file sharing, making them ideal for project-based work and committee communications.

Content Management Systems (CMS)

Internal Blogs and News Portals: Using a CMS to manage an internal blog or news portal allows for the easy publication of updates, stories, and educational content that can foster a sense of community and keep everyone informed.

Social Media and Networking Platforms

Private Groups and Forums: Creating private groups or forums on platforms like Facebook, LinkedIn, or dedicated apps can encourage informal interactions, peer support, and community building among various groups within the university.

Mobile Apps

Custom University Apps: Custom mobile apps can provide personalized access to resources, schedules, notifications, and communications channels, catering to the mobile-first preferences of many students and faculty.

Video Conferencing Tools

Virtual Meetings and Webinars: Tools like Zoom, Microsoft Teams, and Google Meet allow for virtual meetings, lectures, and webinars, facilitating communication and learning in a hybrid or remote environment.

Traditional Communication Channels

Bulletin Boards: Physical and digital bulletin boards can be used for posting important announcements, opportunities, and information about upcoming events, complementing digital communications.

Printed Materials: Newsletters, flyers, and brochures can be effective, especially for reaching stakeholders who prefer traditional communication methods or for distributing in communal areas.

Techniques for Enhancing Internal Communications

Regular Updates and Newsletters: Scheduled communications, such as weekly or monthly newsletters, keep the community informed about recent achievements, news, and upcoming events.

Town Hall Meetings: Regularly scheduled town hall meetings, whether virtual or in-person, offer a forum for leadership to communicate directly with the university community and field questions or concerns.

Feedback Surveys: Conducting regular surveys or having an open feedback mechanism allows members of the university to voice their opinions, concerns, and suggestions, making them feel heard and valued.

Recognition Programs: Implementing programs to recognize and celebrate the achievements of students, faculty, and staff can boost morale and foster a positive campus culture.

Training and Workshops: Providing training sessions or workshops on effective communication practices, tools, and resources can enhance the overall efficiency and effectiveness of internal communications.

By employing a mix of these tools and techniques, universities can create a dynamic and inclusive internal communication strategy that addresses the needs of their diverse community. The key is to maintain a balance between digital and traditional methods, ensuring that all members of the university, regardless of their preferred communication channels or access to technology, are reached and engaged.

CHAPTER TWENTY-THREE

Engaging Faculty and Staff

Engaging faculty and staff effectively is crucial for fostering a positive work environment and achieving the strategic goals of universities. Particularly in India, where higher education institutions grapple with diversity in disciplines, cultures, and languages, engagement strategies need to be nuanced and inclusive. Here are key strategies for engaging faculty and staff in Indian universities:

Transparent and Open Communication

Regular Updates: Keep faculty and staff informed about university developments, changes, and achievements through newsletters, emails, and meetings. Transparency fosters trust and inclusion.

Feedback Channels: Establish open channels for feedback, allowing faculty and staff to voice their opinions, concerns, and suggestions. This could be through surveys, suggestion boxes, or town hall meetings.

Professional Development Opportunities

Continuing Education: Offer opportunities for faculty and staff to pursue further education or professional development courses. This not only aids their personal growth but also enriches the university's academic environment.

Workshops and Seminars: Organize regular workshops and seminars on emerging teaching methods, research methodologies, and technological tools to enhance their skills and knowledge.

Recognition and Rewards

Acknowledgment Programs: Implement programs to recognize and reward the hard work and achievements of faculty and staff. Recognition can be in the form of awards, public acknowledgment, or even a simple thank you note.

Career Advancement: Clearly outline paths for career advancement and make the promotion criteria transparent. Encouraging and supporting career growth can significantly enhance engagement and motivation.

Foster a Collaborative Culture

Interdepartmental Projects: Encourage collaboration on projects or research across different departments. This not only fosters a sense of unity but also promotes interdisciplinary learning and innovation.

Team-building Activities: Organize team-building activities and social events that allow faculty and staff to interact outside of their professional roles, strengthening interpersonal relationships and building a sense of community.

Support Work-Life Balance

Flexible Work Arrangements: Where possible, offer flexible working hours or the option to work remotely. This acknowledges the diverse needs of faculty and staff, promoting a healthier work-life balance.

Wellness Programs: Implement wellness programs that address physical, mental, and emotional health. This could include access to fitness facilities, mental health workshops, and counseling services.

Create an Inclusive Environment

Diversity and Inclusion Initiatives: Actively work to create an inclusive environment that respects and celebrates diversity. This could involve training sessions on diversity and inclusion, celebrating cultural festivals, and ensuring equal opportunities for all.

Safe and Supportive Workplace: Ensure that the university is a safe space for all employees, free from discrimination or harassment. Establish clear policies and a support system for those who may face issues.

Leverage Technology

Digital Tools for Efficiency: Utilize digital tools and platforms to streamline administrative tasks, facilitating more time for teaching, research, and engagement activities.

Online Platforms for Collaboration: Employ online platforms that encourage collaboration and sharing of ideas among faculty and staff, fostering a culture of innovation and shared learning.

By implementing these strategies, universities in India can engage their faculty and staff more effectively, creating a vibrant, collaborative, and supportive academic community. Engaged faculty and staff are more likely to be committed to the institution's vision, contribute to a positive campus atmosphere, and positively impact student success and satisfaction.

CHAPTER TWENTY-FOUR

Student Communications: Ensuring Clarity and Inclusivity

Effective communication with students is paramount for universities, especially in the diverse and dynamic educational landscape of India. Ensuring that messages are clear, inclusive, and accessible to all students, regardless of their background, discipline, or level of study, is crucial for fostering an environment that supports academic success and personal growth. Here's how universities can achieve clarity and inclusivity in student communications.

Understand Your Audience

Diverse Student Body: Recognize the diversity within the student population, including cultural, linguistic, academic, and social differences. Tailoring communication to meet these varied needs enhances understanding and engagement.

Student Needs and Preferences: Regularly gather feedback on students' communication preferences, challenges, and needs through surveys, focus groups, or forums.

Use Clear and Concise Language

Simplicity is Key: Use simple, direct language that is easily understandable to ensure that all students, including those for whom English is a second language, can grasp the message.

Avoid Jargon: Minimize the use of academic jargon or technical terms without clear explanations. When specialized language is necessary, provide definitions or additional context.

Employ Multiple Channels for Communication

Diverse Channels: Utilize a mix of channels to communicate with students, including email, social media, the university website, mobile apps, and traditional bulletin boards. This multi-channel approach ensures that messages reach students through their preferred mediums.

Accessibility Features: Ensure digital communications are accessible, incorporating features such as alt text for images, subtitles for videos, and screen reader-friendly content.

Foster an Inclusive Environment

Cultural Sensitivity: Craft messages that are culturally sensitive and inclusive, reflecting the diverse backgrounds and identities of the student body.

Inclusive Language: Use language that is inclusive of all genders, nationalities, and abilities, avoiding assumptions or stereotypes.

Provide Clear Calls to Action

Guidance and Direction: Clearly state what action, if any, students need to take in response to the communication. Whether it's registering for a class, attending a campus event, or completing a survey, make the steps clear and straightforward.

Support and Resources: Include information on where students can go for help or more information, such as links to relevant resources or contact details for support services.

Encourage Feedback and Dialogue

Two-way Communication: Encourage and facilitate two-way communication, where students feel comfortable voicing their opinions, asking questions, and providing feedback.

Responsive Mechanisms: Implement mechanisms for responding to student inquiries and feedback promptly and effectively, demonstrating that their voices are heard and valued.

Regularly Review and Adapt Communication Strategies

Continuous Improvement: Regularly review the effectiveness of communication strategies, using student feedback and engagement metrics to identify areas for improvement.

Adaptation and Flexibility: Be prepared to adapt communication strategies based on changing student needs, preferences, and the evolving communication landscape.

By prioritizing clarity and inclusivity, universities in India can enhance the effectiveness of their communications with students, promoting a sense of belonging and support. This approach not only aids in academic success but also contributes to a positive and enriching university experience for every student.

Section 7 - Alumni Relations and Fundraising

CHAPTER TWENTY-FIVE

Building a Strong Alumni Network

A robust alumni network is a valuable asset for any university, serving as a testament to the institution's educational quality and community strength. For Indian universities, which are part of a rapidly growing and evolving higher education landscape, building and maintaining a strong alumni network can offer numerous benefits, including mentorship opportunities for current students, financial support through donations, and enhanced reputation. Here's how universities in India can cultivate a vibrant and engaged alumni community.

Develop a Comprehensive Alumni Database

Collect and Update Information: Create a comprehensive database to collect and regularly update alumni contact information, professional achievements, and other relevant details. This database serves as the foundation for all alumni engagement efforts.

Utilize Alumni Management Software: Consider using specialized alumni management software to streamline database management, event planning, and communication.

Engage Alumni through Targeted Communication

Regular Updates: Keep alumni informed about university news, achievements, and events through newsletters, emails, and social media. Tailoring content to different alumni segments based on their interests and graduation years can increase engagement.

Alumni Spotlights: Feature alumni success stories in university publications and on social media platforms to celebrate their achievements and inspire current students.

Organize Networking and Social Events

- **Reunions and Networking Events:** Organize regular reunions, networking events, and social gatherings, both on-campus and in major cities, to facilitate connections among alumni and between alumni and current students.
- **Professional Development Workshops:** Offer workshops, webinars, and guest lectures by distinguished alumni in their fields of expertise, providing valuable learning opportunities for both current students and fellow alumni.

Create Meaningful Opportunities for Involvement

Mentorship Programs: Establish mentorship programs that connect alumni with current students for career guidance, internships, and job placements. This not only benefits students but also allows alumni to give back to their alma mater in a meaningful way.

Advisory Roles: Invite alumni to serve on advisory boards, contribute to curriculum development, or participate in accreditation processes, leveraging their expertise and experience for the university's benefit.

Foster a Culture of Giving Back

Fundraising Campaigns: Launch targeted fundraising campaigns for scholarships, infrastructure projects, or research initiatives. Clearly communicating the impact of these donations can motivate alumni to contribute.

Alumni Giving Programs: Develop specialized giving programs that recognize alumni contributions at various levels, creating a sense of ownership and pride in the university's development.

Leverage Technology for Engagement

Alumni Portal: Develop an online portal or mobile app that serves as a one-stop-shop for alumni to access news, event registrations, mentorship opportunities, and donation platforms.

Social Media Groups: Utilize social media platforms to create alumni groups based on geographic location, academic departments, or extracurricular interests, facilitating easier communication and engagement among alumni with similar interests.

Recognize and Appreciate Alumni Contributions

Alumni Awards: Institute awards to recognize alumni for professional achievements, community service, or contributions to the university, further strengthening their connection to the institution.

Thank You Communications: Regularly express gratitude to alumni for their involvement, support, and contributions, whether through personalized letters, public acknowledgments, or special events.

Building a strong alumni network requires consistent effort, strategic planning, and a genuine commitment to fostering long-term relationships. By implementing these strategies, Indian universities can unlock the full potential of their alumni community, benefiting both the institution and its graduates.

CHAPTER TWENTY-SIX

Strategies for Engaging Alumni

Engaging alumni effectively can significantly benefit universities, fostering a supportive network that contributes to the institution's reputation, development, and the success of its current students. For Indian universities navigating a diverse and expansive educational landscape, crafting thoughtful and inclusive strategies is key to maintaining a vibrant alumni community. Here are several strategies designed to enhance alumni engagement:

1. Personalized Communication

Segment Your Alumni: Divid‾e your alumni database into segments based on factors like graduation year, location, or field of study. This allows for more targeted and relevant communication.

Tailored Messages: Send personalized communications that resonate with specific alumni groups, acknowledging their unique experiences and interests related to the university.

2. Leveraging Digital Platforms

Social Media Engagement: Utilize social media platforms to create alumni groups, share university news, celebrate alumni achievements, and promote events. Regular, interactive posts can keep alumni connected and engaged.

Alumni Portals and Apps: Develop an alumni portal or mobile app offering easy access to alumni directories, event registrations, career resources, and donation opportunities.

3. Networking Opportunities

Alumni Events: Organize regular alumni events, including reunions, networking mixers, and professional development workshops. Both in-person and virtual events can help alumni connect with their peers and the university.

Industry and Interest Groups: Create groups or chapters based on industry sectors or shared interests to facilitate networking and mentorship opportunities among alumni with similar professional backgrounds or hobbies.

4. Lifelong Learning

Continuing Education: Offer alumni access to online courses, webinars, and lectures to encourage lifelong learning and professional growth. This not only benefits alumni but also keeps them connected to the university's academic community.

Access to Campus Resources: Allow alumni to utilize campus facilities and resources, such as libraries, labs, or sports facilities, reinforcing their ongoing relationship with the university.

5. Recognition and Involvement

Alumni Awards and Honors: Recognize outstanding alumni achievements through awards and honors. Highlighting alumni success stories can inspire current students and strengthen the alumni's bond with the university.

Advisory Roles: Invite alumni to serve in advisory capacities, contribute to strategic planning, or participate in panels and discussions. Their expertise and experience can be invaluable assets to the university.

6. Mentorship and Career Support

Mentorship Programs: Establish mentorship programs pairing alumni with current students. These programs can provide valuable guidance, support, and networking opportunities to students while giving alumni a meaningful way to give back.

Career Services: Offer career support services to alumni, including job postings, career counseling, and resume workshops. This support can be a significant resource throughout their professional lives.

7. Philanthropic Engagement

Fundraising Campaigns: Engage alumni in fundraising efforts for scholarships, research initiatives, or capital projects. Clear communication about the impact of their contributions can motivate alumni to donate.

Volunteer Opportunities: Create opportunities for alumni to volunteer their time and skills for university events, community service projects, or student mentorship, fostering a deeper sense of community and commitment.

8. Celebrating University Traditions

Annual Events: Host annual events that celebrate university traditions and milestones. Inviting alumni to participate in these traditions can rekindle fond memories and strengthen their emotional connection to the institution.

Effective alumni engagement requires a multifaceted approach, leveraging technology, personalized communication, and meaningful involvement opportunities. By implementing these strategies, Indian universities can cultivate a thriving alumni community that actively contributes to the institution's legacy and supports its future endeavors.

CHAPTER TWENTY-SEVEN

Communications Strategy for Fundraising Campaigns

Effective communication is the linchpin of successful fundraising campaigns for universities. It's not just about asking for donations; it's about telling a compelling story, building relationships, and articulating the impact of contributions. For Indian universities, which operate within a diverse cultural and economic landscape, crafting a nuanced communications strategy is crucial. Here are strategic elements to consider:

Define Clear Objectives and Audience

Set Specific Goals: Beyond the overall financial target, define what the funds will achieve. Whether it's building new facilities, funding research, scholarships, or endowments, clarity on objectives resonates with potential donors.

Identify Target Audiences: Segment your potential donors into categories such as alumni, parents, corporations, philanthropists, and faculty. Tailor your messaging to resonate with each group's interests and connection to the university.

Craft a Compelling Narrative

Tell a Story: People are moved to donate by emotional narratives that connect them to a cause. Share stories of students, faculty, and research projects that have been impacted by donations, highlighting the difference further contributions can make.

Showcase Impact: Use data and real-life examples to demonstrate the tangible outcomes of donations. Visuals, testimonials, and case studies can make the impact more relatable and compelling.

Utilize a Multi-Channel Approach

Diverse Communication Channels: Employ a mix of channels to reach your audience, including email campaigns, social media, direct mail, phone calls, and in-person events. Consider the preferences and behaviors of your target audience segments when choosing channels.

Consistency Across Channels: Ensure consistent messaging across all platforms, reinforcing the campaign's objectives, stories, and calls to action. Cohesiveness strengthens brand recognition and campaign visibility.

Engage Through Personalized Communication

Personalization: Tailor communications to reflect the recipient's previous interactions, donations, and relationship with the university. Personalized appeals are more likely to elicit a positive response.

Acknowledgment and Appreciation: Recognize and thank donors for their contributions, regardless of the size, through personalized messages, public acknowledgments, or exclusive events.

Leverage Social Proof

Peer Influence: Encourage alumni and donors to share their reasons for donating on social media, creating a ripple effect. Testimonials and endorsements from respected individuals within the community can significantly boost credibility and influence others to contribute.

Matching Gifts: Highlight any matching gift opportunities, where corporations or major donors match contributions from others, doubling the impact of donations and motivating more people to participate.

Make Giving Easy and Transparent

Simplify the Donation Process: Ensure that the process of making a donation is as simple and straightforward as possible, with clear instructions and multiple payment options.

Transparency: Be open about how funds will be used and report back on the progress and outcomes of funded projects. Transparency builds trust and encourages continued support.

Monitor, Evaluate, and Adapt

Track and Measure: Use analytics to monitor the effectiveness of different communication channels and messages. This data can inform adjustments to the strategy in real time to optimize campaign performance.

Feedback Loops: Encourage feedback from donors and potential donors about their communication preferences, motivations for giving, and perceptions of the campaign. This insight can be invaluable for refining current and future fundraising efforts.

A well-crafted communications strategy for fundraising campaigns can transform the philanthropic landscape of a university, turning aspirations into achievements. By engaging donors with compelling narratives, personalized outreach, and transparent processes, Indian universities can foster a culture of giving that supports their mission and vision for the future.

Section 8 – Measuring and Evaluating Your Communications Efforts

CHAPTER TWENTY-EIGHT

Key Performance Indicators (KPIs) for University Communications

In the context of university communications, setting clear Key Performance Indicators (KPIs) is crucial for evaluating effectiveness, guiding strategy, and demonstrating ROI. These metrics help universities, including those in India with their diverse and vast educational landscape, to measure the impact of their communications across various channels and initiatives. Here's a comprehensive look at essential KPIs for university communications.

Website Analytics

Unique Visitors: Tracks the number of distinct individuals visiting your university's website, indicating the reach of your online presence.

Pageviews: The total number of pages viewed. High numbers suggest engaging content, while analyzing the most visited pages can indicate audience interest areas.

Bounce Rate: The percentage of visitors who navigate away from the site after viewing only one page, helping assess the first impression and relevance of content.

Average Session Duration: The average amount of time spent on the site per visit, indicating the engagement level with your content.

Social Media Metrics

Follower Growth: The rate at which your university's social media following increases, indicating brand awareness and appeal.

Engagement Rate: Includes likes, comments, shares, and retweets. High engagement rates suggest that your content resonates with your audience.

Impressions and Reach: Measures how often your content is displayed (impressions) and how many unique users see your content (reach).

Click-Through Rate (CTR): The ratio of users who click on a specific link to the number of total users who view a page, email, or advertisement. It's crucial for assessing the effectiveness of calls-to-action.

Email Marketing Performance

Open Rate: The percentage of recipients who open a given email, indicating the effectiveness of your subject lines and the interest level of your audience.

Click-Through Rate (CTR): Measures how many people clicked on links within the email, reflecting the relevance and appeal of the content.

Conversion Rate: The percentage of email recipients who completed a desired action, such as donating, registering for an event, or applying to a program, indicating the email's effectiveness in driving actions.

Unsubscribe Rate: Tracks the rate at which people opt-out of your email list after receiving an email, which can signal issues with content relevance or frequency.

Public Relations (PR) Metrics

Media Mentions: The number of times your university is mentioned in the media. Tracking both volume and sentiment (positive, neutral, negative) can gauge brand visibility and public perception.

Press Release Pickup: Measures how many and which media outlets have picked up and published your press releases, indicating the effectiveness of your distribution strategy.

Earned Media Value (EMV): An estimate of what the media coverage would have cost if it were paid advertising, providing insight into the value of PR efforts.

Alumni Engagement Metrics

Event Attendance: Tracking attendance at alumni events can measure engagement and the effectiveness of event marketing.

Alumni Donations Rate: The percentage of alumni who donate, which can indicate alumni loyalty and the effectiveness of fundraising communications.

Alumni Newsletter Engagement: Open and click-through rates for emails sent to alumni, providing insights into the relevance and engagement of content targeted at this group.

For Indian universities, aligning these KPIs with specific communications goals and audience segments is essential. Regularly monitoring, analyzing, and adapting based on these metrics can lead to more strategic, effective, and impactful communications efforts.

CHAPTER TWENTY-NINE

Tools and Techniques for Measurement and Analysis

In the evolving landscape of higher education, leveraging tools and techniques for measurement and analysis is essential for universities to gauge the effectiveness of their communications strategies. This approach enables institutions, including those in India, to make data-driven decisions, optimize their outreach, and better meet the needs of their diverse audiences. Here's an overview of the key tools and techniques that can aid in this process.

Web Analytics Tools

Google Analytics: Provides comprehensive insights into website traffic, user behavior, page views, session duration, bounce rate, and conversions. It's instrumental in understanding how visitors interact with your university's website.

Heat Mapping Tools (e.g., Hotjar, Crazy Egg): Offer visual representations of where users click, scroll, and spend time on your site, helping identify the most engaging content and potential areas for improvement.

Social Media Analytics Platforms

Built-in Analytics (e.g., Facebook Insights, Twitter Analytics, LinkedIn Analytics): Social platforms offer native analytics tools that track engagement, follower growth, reach, and the performance of specific posts or campaigns.

Third-Party Social Media Management Tools (e.g., Hootsuite, Buffer, Sprout Social): These tools provide aggregated analytics across multiple social media platforms, making it easier to compare performance across channels and manage campaigns in a centralized dashboard.

Email Marketing Software

Platforms like Mailchimp, Constant Contact, and Campaign Monitor: Offer detailed reports on email campaigns, including open rates, click-through rates, conversion rates, and unsubscribe rates. These insights are crucial for refining email communication strategies.

Survey and Feedback Tools

Online Survey Platforms (e.g., SurveyMonkey, Google Forms): Facilitate the collection of feedback from students, faculty, alumni, and other stakeholders, providing qualitative insights into the effectiveness of communications and areas for improvement.

Net Promoter Score (NPS): A tool used to gauge the loyalty of stakeholder relationships and satisfaction with the university's communications efforts.

Content Performance and SEO Tools

SEO Platforms (e.g., Moz, SEMrush, Ahrefs): These tools offer insights into keyword rankings, backlink profiles, and content performance in search results, helping optimize web content for better visibility and engagement.

Content Management System (CMS) Analytics: Most CMS platforms have built-in analytics that can track the performance of content published on the university's website, including views, engagement, and interaction metrics.

Media Monitoring and Sentiment Analysis Tools

Media Monitoring Services (e.g., Meltwater, Cision): Track mentions of your university across various media outlets, blogs, and forums, providing quantitative and qualitative analysis of media coverage.

Sentiment Analysis Tools: Use natural language processing (NLP) to gauge the sentiment (positive, negative, neutral) of social media mentions, news articles, and other digital content related to your university.

Data Visualization and Reporting Tools

Data Visualization Software (e.g., Tableau, Google Data Studio): These tools help in creating interactive dashboards and visual reports that make it easier to understand and communicate the insights derived from data analysis.

Custom Dashboards: Integrating data from various sources into custom dashboards can provide a holistic view of communications performance across all channels.

Leveraging these tools and techniques allows universities to systematically measure the impact of their communications, identify trends, understand stakeholder needs, and continuously refine their strategies for maximum effectiveness. In the competitive and diverse educational sector of India, such an analytical approach is indispensable for staying ahead and achieving communication excellence.

CHAPTER THIRTY

Adjusting Your Strategy Based on Feedback and Data

For universities, especially those navigating the diverse and dynamic educational landscape of India, continuously refining communication strategies is crucial. Leveraging feedback and data not only enhances engagement with your target audiences but also ensures your communications efforts are aligned with your institution's goals. Here's how universities can adjust their strategies based on feedback and data:

Collect and Analyze Feedback

Surveys and Questionnaires: Regularly distribute surveys to students, faculty, alumni, and other stakeholders to gather feedback on various aspects of your communication efforts. Tools like SurveyMonkey or Google Forms can facilitate this process.

Focus Groups: Organize focus groups with representatives from different segments of your university community to dive deeper into the effectiveness of your communications and gather qualitative insights.

Social Media Listening: Utilize social media monitoring tools to track mentions of your university, gauge sentiment, and understand the conversations happening around your brand.

Utilize Analytics Tools

Website Analytics: Tools like Google Analytics provide valuable insights into website visitor behavior, content engagement, and conversion rates, helping you understand what content resonates with your audience.

Email Analytics: Email marketing platforms offer metrics such as open rates, click-through rates, and conversion rates, allowing you to assess the effectiveness of your email communications.

Social Media Analytics: Platforms like Facebook Insights and Twitter Analytics offer detailed data on engagement, reach, and audience demographics, enabling you to fine-tune your social media strategy.

Identify Areas for Improvement

Content Relevance: If certain types of content consistently underperform in engagement metrics, it may indicate a mismatch with your audience's interests or needs. Use this insight to adjust your content strategy.

Channel Effectiveness: Analyze which communication channels are most effective for reaching your target audiences and consider reallocating resources to prioritize those channels.

Timing and Frequency: Feedback and data can also inform the optimal timing and frequency of your communications, ensuring that your messages are well-received and not overwhelming.

Implement Changes Strategically

Pilot New Approaches: Before rolling out major changes based on feedback and data, pilot new approaches with a smaller segment of your audience to gauge effectiveness and make necessary adjustments.

Communicate Changes: Let your community know how their feedback has contributed to changes in your communication strategy. This not only demonstrates that you value their input but also fosters a sense of community and engagement.

Monitor Results: Continuously monitor the results of any changes implemented, using both qualitative feedback and quantitative data to assess impact.

Foster a Culture of Continuous Improvement

Iterative Process: View the adjustment of your communication strategy as an ongoing, iterative process. Regularly scheduled reviews of feedback and data should inform your strategy, creating a dynamic approach that evolves with your community's needs.

Stakeholder Involvement: Involve various stakeholders in the process of adjusting your strategy. This can include communications team members, faculty, students, and alumni, ensuring a diverse range of perspectives.

By systematically collecting and analyzing feedback and data, universities can make informed decisions to refine their communication strategies. This not only improves the effectiveness of communications but also enhances the overall engagement and satisfaction of the university community, driving towards the achievement of institutional goals.

Section 9 - Case Studies and Best Practices

CHAPTER THIRTY-ONE

Examples of Communications Campaigns

In the dynamic and diverse landscape of Indian higher education, universities often launch various communications campaigns to bolster their reputation, attract students, and foster a sense of community among students, faculty, and alumni. While specifics might vary, successful campaigns usually share common attributes such as clear objectives, creative execution, and effective audience engagement. Here are hypothetical examples of successful communications campaigns in Indian universities that highlight these attributes.

"Green Campus Initiative" Campaign

Objective: To position the university as a leader in sustainability and environmental responsibility.

Execution: The campaign utilized a mix of digital media, on-campus events, and public installations that showcased the university's commitment to green practices. A highlight was a series of engaging videos featuring students and faculty involved in sustainability projects, shared across social media platforms.

Engagement: The campaign encouraged the university community to participate in green initiatives, such as tree planting events and sustainability workshops. It also featured a hashtag, #GreenFutureU, for sharing actions and ideas on social media.

Outcome: Increased participation in sustainability programs, significant media coverage, and a rise in applications from students interested in environmental studies.

"Alumni Success Stories" Series

Objective: To strengthen alumni engagement and inspire current students by highlighting the achievements of the university's alumni.

Execution: This series featured monthly interviews with successful alumni across various fields, sharing their journey from university life to professional success. The stories were shared through the university's newsletter, website, and social media platforms, with each story accompanied by a short, inspirational video.

Engagement: Alumni were invited to submit their own stories or nominate peers, creating a sense of community and pride. The campaign also included Q&A sessions with featured alumni, allowing current students to interact and seek advice.

Outcome: Enhanced alumni contributions, increased mentorship opportunities for students, and higher engagement rates on the university's digital platforms.

"Campus Life Unfiltered" Campaign

Objective: To attract prospective students by providing an authentic look at campus life and the academic environment.

Execution: Utilizing user-generated content, the campaign curated a collection of stories, photos, and videos from students showcasing their daily life, academic projects, and extracurricular activities. This content was shared through a dedicated section on the university website and promoted via social media and email marketing.

Engagement: The campaign encouraged current students to share their experiences using a specific hashtag, fostering a sense of belonging and community. Prospective students could ask questions directly to those featured, providing a personal touch to the recruitment process.

Outcome: An increase in engagement on social media platforms, positive feedback from prospective students, and a noticeable uptick in applications for admission.

"Innovation in Research" Showcase

Objective: To highlight the university's research achievements and attract research collaborations and funding.

Execution: The campaign featured breakthrough research projects and innovations developed at the university. It included detailed articles, researcher interviews, and behind-the-scenes looks at research processes, shared through the university's website, academic forums, and targeted email campaigns to industry partners.

Engagement: Interactive webinars and on-campus showcases were organized, inviting industry experts, potential collaborators, and media to discuss future research directions and partnerships.

Outcome: Strengthened relationships with industry partners, increased media coverage of the university's research projects, and a rise in funding for new research initiatives.

These hypothetical campaigns demonstrate how Indian universities can leverage creative strategies and diverse communication channels to achieve various objectives, from enhancing sustainability efforts and showcasing alumni success to providing insights into campus life and highlighting research innovations. By engaging their target audiences effectively, universities can strengthen their community ties, enhance their reputation, and support their strategic goals.

CHAPTER THIRTY-TWO

Lessons Learned from Communications Failures

Communications failures can be turning points for organizations, including universities, offering valuable lessons that contribute to future successes. These failures often highlight the importance of clarity, transparency, and audience understanding. By examining common pitfalls and integrating these lessons into future strategies, institutions can significantly improve their communications efficacy. Here are key lessons learned from past communications failures in a generalized context:

The Necessity of Clarity and Precision

Lesson: Ambiguous or vague messages canz̄ lead to misunderstandings, confusion, or misinterpretation among the audience. It's crucial to convey information clearly and precisely.

Application: Universities should ensure that all communications, especially those related to policies, programs, and procedures, are straightforward and unambiguous. This might involve simplifying language, avoiding jargon, and providing concrete examples.

The Importance of Audience Segmentation

Lesson: A one-size-fits-all approach to communication often falls short, failing to resonate with or even reaching the intended audience. Understanding and segmenting the audience based on their needs, preferences, and communication habits is essential.

Application: Tailor messages to different segments of the university community (students, faculty, alumni, etc.) using the most appropriate channels and messaging styles for each group.

Timeliness and Proactivity in Crisis Communication

Lesson: Delayed responses or a lack of proactive communication during a crisis can exacerbate the situation, leading to rumors, speculation, and increased distrust among stakeholders.

Application: Develop a crisis communication plan that includes protocols for rapid response, designated spokespersons, and strategies for maintaining open lines of communication throughout the crisis.

Transparency Builds Trust

Lesson: Withholding information or appearing to be less than fully transparent can erode trust and credibility with your audience.

Application: Commit to openness in communications, especially concerning issues or decisions that directly impact the university community. When mistakes are made, acknowledge them openly and outline steps to address and rectify the situation.

Engaging in Two-way Communication

Lesson: Viewing communication as a one-way dissemination of information misses the opportunity for dialogue, feedback, and engagement, which can lead to disconnects between institutions and their audiences.

Application: Foster a culture of two-way communication by encouraging feedback, facilitating discussions, and actively listening to the concerns and suggestions of the university community.

Continuous Monitoring and Adaptation

Lesson: The external environment and the needs of stakeholders evolve, and communications strategies that fail to adapt can become ineffective.

Application: Regularly review and assess the effectiveness of communication strategies, using both quantitative metrics and qualitative feedback, and be prepared to make adjustments in response to changing circumstances and insights.

The Value of Preparedness

Lesson: Being caught off-guard by events or issues that require immediate communication can lead to rushed and poorly executed messages.

Application: Maintain up-to-date communication plans, including templates and protocols for various scenarios, ensuring the university is prepared to communicate effectively under any circumstances.

Cultural Sensitivity Matters

Lesson: Messages that fail to consider the cultural, social, or personal contexts of the audience can lead to offense, misunderstanding, or alienation.

Application: Ensure that communications are culturally sensitive, inclusive, and respectful, taking into account the diverse backgrounds and perspectives within the university community.

By learning from past communication failures, universities can enhance their strategies to foster a more informed, engaged, and cohesive community. These lessons underscore the importance of clear, timely, and audience-centric communication practices in building trust and achieving institutional goals.

CHAPTER THIRTY-THREE

Best Practices from Global Higher Education Institutions

Global higher education institutions have pioneered numerous successful communication strategies, setting benchmarks for engaging academic communities and stakeholders effectively. These best practices, drawn from universities worldwide, offer valuable insights that can be adapted and implemented by institutions aiming to enhance their communication efforts. Here are some noteworthy strategies:

Embracing Digital Transformation

Interactive Websites: Top universities have developed dynamic, user-friendly websites that serve as comprehensive portals for information, engagement, and services.

Social Media Excellence: Successful institutions utilize social media not just for broadcasting news but for engaging with students, alumni, and the global academic community through interactive content, live sessions, and community discussions.

Personalized Communication

Segmented Email Campaigns: By segmenting their audience based on interests, behaviors, and academic focus, universities can tailor their emails to ensure relevance and increase engagement.

Customized Portal and Apps: Some institutions offer personalized student portals and mobile apps that aggregate relevant information, notifications, and learning resources based on the student's course of study and interests.

Leveraging Content Marketing

Storytelling: Sharing compelling stories of student achievements, research breakthroughs, and community initiatives helps institutions connect emotionally with their audiences, fostering a sense of pride and belonging.

Video Content: Utilizing video for campus tours, student testimonials, and behind-the-scenes looks at academic and extracurricular activities has proven effective in engaging prospective and current students.

Building a Strong Community Online

Alumni Networks: Platforms that facilitate networking, mentorship, and professional development among alumni not only keep graduates connected to the institution but also encourage giving back in various forms.

Virtual Events: Hosting webinars, online conferences, and virtual meetups expands the institution's reach, allowing for greater participation from around the globe.

Prioritizing Transparency and Responsiveness

Open Forums and AMAs (Ask Me Anything): Institutions that organize regular sessions where students and staff can ask questions directly to the administration demonstrate a commitment to transparency and accountability.

Crisis Communication: Effective crisis communication plans, including timely updates and clear information during emergencies, build trust and confidence among campus communities.

Encouraging Two-way Communication

Feedback Mechanisms: Implementing formal and informal channels for feedback ensures that the voices of students, faculty, and staff are heard and considered in decision-making processes.

Participatory Decision-making: Some institutions involve student and staff representatives in governance and decision-making processes, enhancing the sense of community and shared purpose.

Continuous Improvement through Data

Analytics and Measurement: Successful universities continually measure the impact of their communication strategies through analytics, adjusting tactics based on data-driven insights to improve engagement and outcomes.

Benchmarking: Comparing communication strategies and outcomes with peer institutions helps identify areas for improvement and innovative practices to adopt.

By adopting and adapting these global best practices, universities can not only improve the effectiveness of their communications but also enhance engagement, community spirit, and institutional reputation. Each strategy highlights the importance of understanding and responding to the needs and preferences of the university community, leveraging technology, and committing to transparency and inclusivity.

Section 10 – Future of Communications in Indian Universities

CHAPTER THIRTY-FOUR

Emerging Trends in Higher Education Communications

The landscape of higher education communications is continually evolving, influenced by technological advancements, changing societal expectations, and the dynamic nature of the global education sector. Recognizing and adapting to these trends is crucial for universities, especially in rapidly developing educational environments like India, to effectively engage with their diverse stakeholders. Here are some emerging trends that are shaping the future of communications in higher education:

Digital and Social Media Integration

Omnichannel Approach: Universities are adopting an omnichannel approach to communications, ensuring a seamless and consistent experience across various digital platforms, including social media, email, and mobile apps.

Social Media Storytelling: Leveraging social media stories and live features has become a popular way to share campus life, events, and achievements in real-time, fostering a sense of immediacy and connection.

Personalization and Customization

AI-driven Personalization: Artificial Intelligence (AI) and machine learning are being used to personalize communication, tailoring messages based on individual user behaviors, preferences, and engagement history.

Customized Content: Universities are creating more customized content that speaks directly to specific groups within their audience, such as prospective students, current students, alumni, or donors.

Visual and Interactive Content

Augmented Reality (AR) and Virtual Reality (VR): AR and VR technologies are being used for virtual campus tours, interactive learning experiences, and engaging prospective students in innovative ways.

Video Content: The use of video content continues to grow, with universities producing high-quality videos for marketing, teaching, and engagement, including mini-documentaries, student vlogs, and instructional content.

Data-driven Strategies

Analytics and Metrics: There is an increasing emphasis on using analytics to guide communication strategies, with universities analyzing data on engagement, reach, and conversion to refine their messaging and tactics.

Feedback Loops: Implementing systematic feedback mechanisms to gather insights from the university community and stakeholders, allowing for real-time adjustments to communication strategies.

Focus on Authenticity and Transparency

Real Voices: Highlighting the authentic voices and stories of students, faculty, and alumni, rather than relying solely on polished marketing messages, to build credibility and trust.

Crisis Communication: Developing proactive and transparent communication strategies for crisis management, emphasizing openness and regular updates during challenging times.

Sustainability and Social Responsibility

Green Communications: An increasing focus on sustainability, with universities communicating their commitment to environmental causes and incorporating eco-friendly practices into their operations and messaging.

Community Engagement: Universities are highlighting their role in social responsibility initiatives, community service, and contributions to societal challenges, aligning their communications with broader social values.

Inclusive and Accessible Communications

Diversity and Inclusion: Prioritizing communications that reflect diversity, equity, and inclusion, ensuring that content and messaging are accessible and resonant with a diverse global audience.

Accessibility Technologies: Implementing technologies and practices to make communications accessible to all, including individuals with disabilities, through captioning, sign language interpretation, and accessible website designs.

These emerging trends underscore the need for universities to be adaptable, innovative, and responsive to the changing landscape of higher education communications. By embracing these trends, universities can enhance their engagement, reach, and impact, effectively connecting with their communities in meaningful ways.

CHAPTER THIRTY-FIVE

Integrating New Technologies in University Communications

Integrating new technologies into university communications strategies is not just about staying current; it's about enhancing engagement, streamlining processes, and opening up new avenues for interaction within the academic community. Here's how universities, including those in India, can leverage emerging technologies to bolster their communications efforts:

Artificial Intelligence and Chatbots

Personalized Interactions: AI-driven chatbots can provide instant, personalized responses to student inquiries on university websites or social media platforms, improving the user experience and freeing up staff for more complex tasks.

Automated Messaging: Use AI to automate routine communications, such as reminders for application deadlines, registration dates, or event notifications, ensuring timely and consistent communication.

Augmented Reality (AR) and Virtual Reality (VR)

Virtual Campus Tours: Utilizing VR, universities can offer immersive virtual tours, allowing prospective students from around the globe to explore campuses, classrooms, and facilities as if they were physically present.

Enhanced Learning Materials: AR can bring textbooks and learning materials to life, providing interactive experiences that can enhance understanding and retention of information.

Blockchain Technology

Secure Credential Verification: Blockchain can securely store academic credentials, allowing for easy verification by employers or other institutions, thereby streamlining the graduate verification process and reducing fraud.

Decentralized Education Records: Implement a system for students to access and share their academic records securely and easily, facilitating mobility and lifelong learning.

Big Data and Analytics

Data-Driven Decision Making: Leverage big data to analyze trends in student behavior, preferences, and engagement, informing more targeted and effective communication strategies.

Predictive Analytics: Use analytics to predict student needs, potential challenges, and engagement opportunities, allowing for proactive rather than reactive communications.

Internet of Things (IoT)

Smart Campus Initiatives: Implement IoT devices across the campus to collect data on facility usage, environmental conditions, and resource consumption, which can be communicated to the campus community to promote sustainability initiatives.

Enhanced Safety Communications: Use IoT devices for real-time safety monitoring and alerts, ensuring swift communication in emergency situations.

Social Media Innovations

Social Listening Tools: Utilize social listening tools to monitor mentions of the university across social media platforms, gaining insights into student sentiment and identifying opportunities for engagement.

Live Streaming: Leverage live streaming capabilities on platforms like Facebook, Instagram, and YouTube to broadcast events, lectures, and Q&A sessions, engaging with the university community in real time.

Podcasts and Audio Platforms

Educational Podcasts: Create podcasts featuring lectures, interviews with faculty and alumni, or discussions on current academic research, making content accessible to a wider audience.

Audio Platforms for Community Building: Utilize audio platforms like Clubhouse for live discussions and networking among students, faculty, alumni, and industry professionals.

Mobile Applications

Custom University Apps: Develop mobile applications that aggregate essential university services, resources, and communications in one place, offering convenience and personalized experiences for students, faculty, and alumni.

By strategically integrating these new technologies into their communications strategies, universities can not only enhance the effectiveness and reach of their messaging but also significantly enrich the academic and campus experience for their communities.

CHAPTER THIRTY-SIX

Preparing for the Future: Skills, Competencies, and Mindsets

As the landscape of higher education evolves, so too do the demands on students, faculty, and administrators. Preparing for the future in such a dynamic environment requires not only a focus on current academic and professional skills but also on developing the competencies and mindsets that will enable individuals to navigate and succeed in a rapidly changing world. Here's a look at the essential skills, competencies, and mindsets needed for the future in higher education contexts:

Adaptive Learning and Flexibility

Continuous Learning: Cultivate a culture of lifelong learning, encouraging students and staff to continually update their knowledge and skills in response to changing demands and opportunities.

Flexibility: Develop the ability to adapt to new situations and challenges, adjusting strategies and approaches as needed.

Digital Literacy and Technological Proficiency

Digital Fluency: Ensure that all members of the university community are comfortable using digital tools and platforms, understanding not just how to use technology but how it can be leveraged to achieve specific goals.

Emerging Technologies: Stay informed about developments in AI, blockchain, VR/AR, and other emerging technologies, exploring how they can be integrated into teaching, learning, and administrative processes.

Critical Thinking and Problem Solving

Analytical Skills: Enhance the ability to analyze information, assess situations from multiple perspectives, and make informed decisions.

Innovative Problem Solving: Encourage creative and innovative approaches to problem-solving, emphasizing the importance of finding novel solutions to complex challenges.

Communication and Collaboration

Effective Communication: Strengthen written, oral, and digital communication skills, ensuring clear and effective exchanges across various mediums and platforms.

Teamwork and Collaboration: Promote collaborative skills, including the ability to work effectively in diverse teams, leveraging the strengths of team members to achieve common goals.

Emotional Intelligence and Interpersonal Skills

Empathy and Understanding: Foster empathy and the ability to understand and relate to the emotions and experiences of others, enhancing personal relationships and team dynamics.

Conflict Resolution: Develop skills in negotiation and conflict resolution, enabling individuals to navigate disagreements and challenges constructively.

Global Awareness and Cultural Competence

Cultural Awareness: Cultivate an understanding of and appreciation for cultural differences, preparing students and staff to operate effectively in a globalized world.

Ethical Reasoning: Promote ethical thinking and decision-making, emphasizing the importance of considering the broader implications of one's actions.

Leadership and Management Competencies

Strategic Leadership: Develop leadership skills that emphasize vision, strategic thinking, and the ability to inspire and guide others toward achieving long-term goals.

Change Management: Equip leaders and administrators with the skills to manage change effectively, including the ability to communicate changes, engage stakeholders, and navigate the uncertainties of transformation.

Resilience and Well-being

Personal Resilience: Encourage practices that build personal resilience, such as mindfulness, stress management, and the cultivation of a growth mindset.

Mental Health Awareness: Increase awareness and understanding of mental health issues, providing support and resources to ensure the well-being of the university community.

Preparing for the future in higher education involves a comprehensive approach that combines the development of hard skills with soft skills and mindsets. By focusing on these areas, universities can equip their students, faculty, and staff with the capabilities needed to thrive in an ever-changing global landscape.

Appendices

CHAPTER THIRTY-SEVEN

Glossary of Terms

This glossary provides definitions for common terms used in the context of university communications, helping to clarify concepts and practices essential to effective communication within higher education institutions.

#A

- **Alumni:** Graduates or former students of a university or college.

- **Analytics:** The systematic computational analysis of data or statistics used to measure and interpret the performance of digital communications.

#B

- **Brand Identity:** The visible elements of a brand, such as color, design, and logo, that identify and distinguish the brand in consumers' minds.

- **Bulletin Board:** A physical or digital board for posting notices, announcements, and information for public view.

#C

- **Content Management System (CMS):** Software that enables users to create, manage, and modify content on a website without the need for specialized technical knowledge.

- **Crisis Communication:** Strategies and practices employed to communicate effectively during a crisis situation, managing information dissemination and public perception.

#D

- **Digital Literacy:** The ability to find, evaluate, and communicate information through digital platforms and technologies.

- **Donor Engagement:** The process of building and maintaining relationships with individuals or organizations that donate funds to the university.

#E

- **Email Marketing:** The use of email to promote events, share news, or solicit donations, engaging with an audience through direct communication.

- **Engagement Rate:** A metric used to measure the level of interaction with content on social media or other digital platforms, typically expressed as a percentage.

#F

- **Feedback Mechanism:** A process or system through which feedback is collected from stakeholders, often used to improve services or communications.

#I

- **Internal Communications:** Communications efforts directed within the organization, aimed at employees or members, to inform, engage, and align them with the organization's goals.

- **Internet of Things (IoT):** The interconnection via the internet of computing devices embedded in everyday objects, enabling them to send and receive data.

#K

- **Key Performance Indicator (KPI):** A measurable value that demonstrates how effectively a company or organization is achieving key objectives.

#M

- **Media Relations:** The practice of managing and cultivating a positive relationship with the media and handling all communications to the press.

- **Mobile Optimization:** The process of adjusting your website content to ensure that visitors accessing the site from mobile devices have an experience optimized for the device.

#P

- **Press Release:** An official statement issued to newspapers and other media for the purpose of providing information, an official announcement, or making a public statement.

- **Public Relations (PR):** The professional maintenance of a favorable public image by an organization or a famous person.

#S

- **Search Engine Optimization (SEO):** The process of optimizing digital content so that a search engine likes to show it as a top result for searches of a certain keyword.

- **Social Media Analytics:** Tools and platforms that analyze the performance of social media content and campaigns, providing insights into engagement, reach, and audience behavior.

#T

- **Target Audience:** A specific group of people identified as the intended recipient of a message or campaign, often characterized by specific demographics or interests.

- **Two-way Communication:** A form of communication where information flows in two directions, allowing for feedback and interaction between the sender and receiver.

Understanding these terms can enhance clarity and improve the effectiveness of communications strategies within universities, ensuring that all stakeholders are engaged and informed in a meaningful way.

CHAPTER THIRTY-EIGHT

Communications Checklists

Pre-Planning

- Define objectives and goals.
- Identify and segment target audiences.
- Develop key messages for each audience segment.

Planning

- Select strategies and tactics for communication.
- Choose channels and tools appropriate for each tactic.
- Create a detailed timeline for all activities.
- Prepare a budget, allocating resources to each element of the plan.
- Establish KPIs for measuring success.

Execution

- Develop content calendars for social media, email campaigns, etc.
- Design and produce necessary materials (e.g., graphics, video).

- Schedule and distribute content according to the timeline.
- Monitor engagement and adjust tactics as necessary.

Post-Execution

- Measure results against KPIs.
- Gather feedback from target audiences and stakeholders.
- Evaluate the overall effectiveness of the communication efforts.
- Document lessons learned and best practices for future communications.

Crisis Communication

- Identify potential crisis scenarios.
- Develop messaging and action plans for each scenario.
- Train spokespersons and communications team on crisis communication.
- Test and refine crisis communication plans regularly.

This checklist provides a structured approach to communications planning, helping university communications teams to execute their strategies effectively. Following this teams can ensure that their communications are coherent, targeted, and impactful.

CHAPTER THIRTY-NINE

List of Useful Resources and Tools

This list provides a curated selection of resources and tools tailored to meet the unique communication, administrative, and operational needs of Indian universities. These tools can enhance efficiency, engagement, and outreach efforts, while addressing the challenges of managing diverse stakeholders.

1. Digital Communication Platforms

- **Hootsuite/Buffer:** Social media management tools to schedule and monitor posts across multiple platforms, especially useful for engaging a diverse student and alumni audience.
- **Mailchimp/SendinBlue:** Email marketing platforms for sending newsletters, announcements, and event invitations.
- **Zoho Campaigns/Merrito:** An Indian-origin email marketing solution with cost-effective options tailored for academic institutions.

2. Website and Content Management

- **WordPress/Drupal:** Popular CMS platforms for building and maintaining user-friendly university websites.
- **TallyFox:** A knowledge management platform for organizing and sharing academic and administrative resources.
- **Crowdsource Tools (Google Workspace):** Tools like Google Drive, Docs, and Sheets for collaborative projects and administrative coordination.

3. Analytics and SEO

- **Google Analytics:** To track website traffic, user behavior, and campaign effectiveness.
- **SimilarWeb:** Useful for understanding digital traffic and benchmarking against similar institutions in India.

4. Virtual Events and Learning

- **Zoom / Google Meet:** Reliable platforms for hosting webinars, online classes, and virtual events.
- **Moodle:** An open-source learning management system widely adopted by Indian universities for online education and communication.
- **Airmeet:** An India-based platform for organizing virtual events like career fairs, alumni meetups, and academic conferences.

5. Social Media and Online Engagement

- **Instagram / Twitter:** For real-time updates, student engagement, and creating vibrant university communities.
- **Canva:** A simple tool for designing social media posts, flyers, and infographics that resonate with Indian students.

6. Alumni Management and Networking

- **Vaave:** A dedicated alumni networking platform tailored for Indian universities.
- **Graduway:** A robust global alumni networking tool that can also be customized for Indian institutions.
- **LinkedIn Alumni Features:** For creating university-specific groups and fostering professional networking.

7. Feedback and Surveys

- **Typeform:** For creating engaging surveys to gather student and faculty feedback.
- **SurveyMonkey:** Widely used for collecting feedback on courses, events, and administrative services.
- **Forms by Zoho:** An India-based alternative for creating customizable online forms.

8. Fundraising and Donations

- **Ketto:** A crowdfunding platform that Indian universities can use to raise funds for specific initiatives.
- **ImpactGuru:** Another India-based platform for crowdfunding campaigns.
- **GiveIndia:** For facilitating donations to educational causes within India.

9. Public Relations and Media Monitoring

- **PR Newswire:** To distribute press releases across India and internationally.
- **Brandwatch/Meltwater:** Media monitoring tools to track mentions and sentiment around your university.
- **Social Mention:** Free tools for tracking social media conversations related to your institution.

10. Project Management and Collaboration

- **Slack/Microsoft Teams:** Platforms for team collaboration, file sharing, and internal communication.
- **Trello/Asana:** Project management tools to streamline workflows and task delegation.
- **Zoho Projects:** An India-based alternative for managing university projects effectively.

11. Video Production and Editing

- **Adobe Premiere Pro/Final Cut Pro/Wondershare Filmora:** For professional video editing and promotional material creation.

- **Kinemaster / InShot:** Affordable and mobile-friendly tools for quick editing of videos, ideal for social media.
- **Veed.io:** For creating subtitles, overlays, and quick edits on videos targeted at student engagement.

12. *Career Services and Job Portals*

- **Naukri Campus:** A job portal dedicated to campus placements and career services in India.
- **Handshake:** For connecting students and alumni with employers globally.
- **Internshala:** An internship platform popular among Indian students.

13. *Legal and Compliance*

- **MCGM Portal (University Grants Commission):** For staying updated with UGC regulations and guidelines.
- **Airtable:** Useful for managing compliance-related data and tracking government mandates.

14. *Student-Centric Tools*

- **Unibuddy:** A peer-to-peer platform where prospective students can connect with current students to understand university life.
- **TCS iON:** A suite of digital tools by Tata Consultancy Services for managing admissions, assessments, and student lifecycle processes.

End Note

The field of university communications is ever-evolving, shaped by advancements in technology, changing audience expectations, and the dynamic nature of higher education itself. This handbook has been designed as a comprehensive resource for Indian universities, offering insights, tools, and strategies to enhance communication efforts across diverse platforms and audiences.

As you apply the principles, strategies, and best practices outlined here, remember that effective communication is not just about delivering messages—it is about building connections, fostering trust, and inspiring action. Whether you're engaging with students, faculty, alumni, or external stakeholders, the ultimate goal is to create a cohesive narrative that reflects your institution's values, vision, and aspirations.

We hope this handbook serves as a valuable companion in your journey to improve and innovate university communications. Embrace the challenges, leverage the opportunities, and continue to adapt and grow as you contribute to the transformative power of higher education.

Here's to building bridges, amplifying voices, and shaping the future—one message at a time.

Dr. Divya Gupta
Author